CONFLICTED POWER

CONFLICTED POWER

Obama's US Foreign and Strategic Policy in a Shifting World Order

Zubaida Rasul-Ronning

authorHOUSE®

AuthorHouse™
1663 Liberty Drive
Bloomington, IN 47403
www.authorhouse.com
Phone: 1-800-839-8640

Published by AuthorHouse   09/25/2012

ISBN: 978-1-4772-7185-8 (sc)
ISBN: 978-1-4772-7184-1 (hc)
ISBN: 978-1-4772-7183-4 (e)

Library of Congress Control Number: 2012917360

Any people depicted in stock imagery provided by Thinkstock are models, and such images are being used for illustrative purposes only.
Certain stock imagery © Thinkstock.

This book is printed on acid-free paper.

Contents

Introduction

"If Iran ever intended to open its nuclear program for inspection, the lack of confidence created by US' cyber warfare initiative conclusively put an end to it, further convincing the Iranian leadership of the malevolence of the P5+1 and the US in particular."

When Barack Hussein Obama came to power in 2008, he was elected on the hopes, struggles and aspirations of generations of Americans, who looked to him to introduce a more progressive US approach in foreign and strategic relations, and perhaps a more magnanimous global leadership. He was awarded the Nobel Peace Prize in 2009 for "promoting international diplomacy and cooperation between peoples . . . (and) a world without nuclear weapons".

The world effectively heaved a huge sigh of relief when George W. Bush completed his term and the first African-American president of the United States took the oath of office. The expectation, as stated by the Nobel Peace Prize Committee, was that Obama would invest in his declared vision of a new era of cooperation and peace in the world. However, it was not till October 2011 that Obama announced the withdrawal of all US troops by end of the same year, and it was not until May 2012 that Obama agreed to a longer-term strategic commitment to the development and stabilization of Afghanistan. Then followed expanded conflicts in Libya and Syria, and growing tensions with Iran on its alleged nuclear program, creating the space for analysis of President Obama's foreign policy.

Drone Warfare

Contrary to what might have been expected, one immediate outcome of Obama's ascent to the White House was the significant increase of the use of **drone technology** to target Taliban and insurgent forces, including Al

Qaeda in Pakistan. Wikipedia presents a good analysis of the these drone strikes:

1) US drone strike statistics estimate bythe New America Foundation analysis of newspaper articles.[1]

Year	Number of Attacks	Number Killed	
		Min.	Max.
2004	1	4	5
2005	2	6	7
2006	2	23	23
2007	4	56	77
2008	33	274	314
2009	53	369	725
2010	118	607	993
2011	70	378	536
2012	28	162	207
Total	311	1,879	2,887

2) **US drone strike statistic based on months of research by a team of journalists of the Bureau of Investigative Journalism:[**

- Total reported killed: 2,520-3,240
- Civilians reported killed: 482-849
- Children reported killed: 175
- Total reported injured: 1,200-1,326
- Strikes under the Bush Administration: 52
- Strikes under the Obama Administration: 284
- Total strikes: 336

Nuclear Disarmament and Cyber Warfare

One of President Obama's key visions that earned him the Nobel Peace Prize was of investing in global and mutual nuclear disarmament. In

---

[1]   http://en.wikipedia.org/wiki/New_America_Foundation

April 2010, President Obama and Russian President Medvedev sign a comprehensive new arms reduction pact that pledged both countries to reduce the stockpile of nuclear weapons and also agreed mutual commitments to new verification procedures concerning the number and type of nuclear weapons they possess[2]. By so doing, President Obama fulfilled one key aspiration associated with his election: making the world a safer place.

It was therefore more shocking that in the next few months in office, President Obama ordered the CIA, working primarily with Israel and UK, to significantly scale up *cyber warfare*, in a cyber attack campaign aimed at crippling Iran's nuclear program.

Cyber warfare first emerged during the years of the George W. Bush presidency as an exploratory response to the increasing challenge and power of cyber-hacking and allied concerns over cyber security. However, it was President Obama who authorized the active use of cyber warfare research conducted under President Bush, as one part of a covert campaign to limit if not disable, Iran's nuclear program[3]. Initiatives such as "*Olympic Games*" and "*Flame*" deployed against Iran, constituted a new horizon in strategic warfare that ranked on the same level of strategic gamesmanship as the decision to use nuclear weapons by President Truman or to use chemical warfare in South East Asia; concretely President Obama introduced cyber warfare as a legitimate tool of war, a tool that could be easily used by states and individuals without the necessity of investing in armies, military hardware or governmental decision-making.

The most serious impact of Obama's decision to scale-up cyber warfare was the total loss of confidence by that country in the ongoing nuclear program negotiations with the P5+1 (the US, UK, France, Russia and China, all permanent members of the Security Council, and Germany). If Iran ever intended to open its nuclear program for inspection, the lack of confidence created by US' cyber warfare initiative conclusively put an end

---

[2] http://www.washingtonpost.com/wp-dyn/content/article/2010/04/08/AR2010040801677.html

[3] http://thecaucus.blogs.nytimes.com/2012/06/01/obamas-counterterrorism-actions-complicate-republican-strategy/

to it, further convincing the Iranian leadership of the malevolence of the P5+1 and the US in particular.

Iran is an open dossier and, in this context, it remains to be seen how President Obama will control and contain the growing military and political independence of Israel. The linkage between the nuclear status of Israel and the pursuit of a nuclear program by Iran might need to be considered as an integral aspect of effective negotiation (*see section on Iran and Israel, page 23*).[4]

End Games: Concretizing the Fight Against Terrorism

Perhaps Obama's most striking leadership move was to approve a risky mission by US special forces to take out Osama Bin Laden.

Based on local intelligence and a last-minute tip-off by a Pakistani doctor[5], President Obama acted on intelligence reports pinpointing the location of Osama Bin Laden. He ordered a risky mission without consulting or informing host country Pakistan. On 2 May 2011, President Obama took to the airwaves to announce that the US had mounted a mission in the Pakistani city of Abbotsabad and had captured and killed Osama Bin Laden in a daring raid. In the process, the US also confiscated valuable computer and paper documentation that would subsequently provide intelligence analysts with a wealth of information on the internal workings and deployments of the larger Al-Qaeda network. The killing of Osama Bin Laden is undoubtedly the crown jewel of the Obama presidency in eliminating global terrorism and in showing himself to be an active commander-in-chief. Since then, a number of other key high-level terrorism targets have also been taken out by targeted drone attacks in Pakistan, Yemen and elsewhere.

The Bin Laden killing, however marked a serious breaking point in the US-Pakistan relationship and, from the Pakistani point of view,

---

4   http://www.nytimes.com/2012/06/01/world/middleeast/obama-ordered-wave-of-cyberattacks-against-iran.html?pagewanted=all

5   http://www.csmonitor.com/World/terrorism-security/2012/0524/Pakistan-to-US-Respect-our-decision-to-sentence-CIA-informant

constituted a breach of the US-Pakistan partnership in fighting terrorism and of Pakistan's sovereignty. The US, apologetic but exposing their lack of confidence in Pakistani integrity in bing s safe haven for extremists and providing refuge to Bin Laden, finally exposed the duplicity of the Pakistanis.

Although healing slowly for the time being, this relationship is in its final stages as neither the US nor Pakistan can continue to avoid the lies and the hidden agendas on which that strategic military and intelligence relationship is based: the instrumentalisation of Pakistan in the decades old war in Afghanistan since the occupation of that country by the Soviet Union; the increasing support of Pakistan for global terrorist networks such as Al-Qaeda and the Haqqani network; the growing political instability in Pakistan; and the growing cohesion between US and India as a counter-weight relationship. All these have shifted the balance in the US-Pakistan-India relationship against Pakistan. Pakistan is looking for redemption in its reinvigorated relationship with China, including through such innovative economic aspects as a contract with the Chinese to build and develop the Pakistani Arabian Gulf port of Gwadar *(see section on Pakistan, page 38)*.

These shifting alliances however, do not diminish but exacerbate the fragility of Pakistan's nuclear status and substantially increase the possibility of Pakistani nuclear weapons falling under terrorist control. In this sense, Pakistan and not Iran[6] poses the imminent global nuclear threat. This truth about Pakistan's susceptibility to becoming a nuclear "rogue power" has not been acknowledged by President Obama, and while the assassination of Osama Bin Laden is a victory for President Obama's war on terrorism, it has increased the insecurity in Pakistan vis-à-vis the US relationship. One important outcome of this insecurity will be the further alienation of the ruling elite, and potentially, this may push Pakistan into further state fragility, exacerbating the danger of it becoming a rogue nuclear state.

---

[6]   http://abcnews.go.com/Politics/osama-bin-laden-dead-president-obama-full-remarks/story?id=13506069#.UDo2fkKhDFI

As a result, the world may be more vulnerable and susceptible to nuclear terrorism. [7]

Promoting International Diplomacy: The Obama Wars and Interventions

> *"The killing of Osama Bin Laden is undoubtedly the crown jewel of the Obama presidency in eliminating global terrorism and in showing himself to be an active commander-in-chief."*

The most striking outcome of the first Obama presidency has been a significant scaling up of the insecurity and instability in the Middle East. While it pales in comparison to the Arab perception of President George W. Bush's Iraq campaign, there is a firm impression globally that the Arab Spring has been promoted and prodded by a combination of US and European covert operations and financing, and a stampeding of the UN Security Council by the US to push through legitimization of a systemic "regime change" agenda[8] in the Middle East.

The Tunisian revolution which toppled long-time dictator Ben-Ali was welcomed by all except France, who had supported Ben-Ali's decades-old tyrannical reign. The US had little impact on the actual revolution but, after its success, has cautiously courted the emergent political order in restoring democracy through elections and economic progress.

The revolutions in Yemen and Egypt both, however, exposed the purposeful US policy stretching over decades of supporting Saleh and Mubarak in dictatorial rule over their peoples. Even when the people's revolution in Egypt was in the final stages of succeeding, the US continued to work to strengthen military rule over that country. In Yemen, the US played a less than honorable role in not supporting the opposition and not pushing

---

[7]   http://www.iss.europa.eu/publications/detail/article/us-strategic-interests-in-south-asia-what-not-to-do-with-pakistan/;

[8]   http://www.thebureauinvestigates.com/2012/03/29/yemen-reported-us-covert-actions-since-2001/
http://en.wikipedia.org/wiki/Covert_United_States_foreign_regime_change_actions

Saleh to step down. Today, Yemen is still struggling to emerge from the control and nepotism of Saleh-era military and political elements that probably are still being financed and supported by the US.

Obama's decision to work with the UK and France in pushing for a Security Council sanctioned NATO intervention in enforcing a no-fly zone over Libya, had one positive outcome: the liberation of Libya from the dictatorial rule of Muanmar Gaddafi. On the negative side, what was perceived as a full authorization for unmitigated and indiscriminate violence quickly tumbled that country into vigilante actions and a complete breakdown and disrespect for the rule of law. Uncontrolled and unsubstantiated private vendettas against ex-Gaddafi regime workers at all levels of governance degraded the liberation into free-for-all violent recrimination.

Lack of controls over significant national weapons and ammunition stockpiles meant that the smuggling of Libyan weapons further south to West Africa resulted in the *de facto* partition of Mali into two, with the installation of an Al-Qaeda state in the north (*see section on Middle East page 1 and Africa page 49*). Next in line is the Islamic Northern Nigeria, while Libyan weapons have been reported as far south as Cote D'Ivoire. The US and NATO made no attempt to support the Libyans in safeguarding their weapons and ammunition, and by not doing so, teasing precipitating the conditions for falling dominoes of simmering conflicts in West Africa.

Syria and Bahrain are both still in phases of active conflict. In Bahrain, US military and political support to the ruling dictatorship continues with total disregard for the significant human rights violations perpetrated against Bahraini people (*see section on Bahrain, page 13*). In Syria, US surrogates Saudi Arabia and Qatar have been progressively increasing monetary support to a massive insurgent war since the bombing death of Rafic Hariri on 14 February 2005 in Lebanon, and to the increase in pressure on Iran to comply with US demands to shut down their nuclear program. While the aim of facilitating access of Syrian people to democratic political processes is a valid and shared objective, the irresolute US policy of not taking direct supportive action, but vocally supporting the objective of regime change in Syria continues to result in a lack of international consensus to end the violence resulting in unacceptable civilian deaths in Syria.

In relation to Syria, Yemen and Bahrain, I question President Obama's contribution to promoting cooperation amongst people while enhancing international diplomacy as a means of making our world safer. While President Obama did conclusively end the occupation by allied forces of Iraq, and he has set a definitive deadline for withdrawal of US forces from Afghanistan, he has also initiated or directly sponsored unacceptable levels of instability in the Middle East. Under Obama's watch, the CIA and other US secret agencies have expanded their program of work—globally, but particularly in the Middle East, raising significant questions about the intent of President Obama's foreign and strategic policy.

Obama's Foreign Policy Refocus: Asia-Pacific

While closing engagements in Iraq and Afghanistan, President Obama has refocused US foreign and strategic policy from the Middle East to the Asia-Pacific. This has underscored the emerging congruence between the US and India, Australia and New Zealand, in part as a response to China's more aggressive Pacific military and economic policy. This also shifts emphasis from the Mediterranean and Atlantic Ocean to the Arabian Gulf and the Indian and Pacific Oceans. While this is perceived as a challenge by China, the US is already working through its allies in the region to tease the many land and sea disputes that remain unresolved in the South China Sea and the Pacific (*see section on China and Asia, page 82*).

With the shifting focus to Asia-Pacific, Obama has made perhaps the most definitive change in US foreign policy since the declaration of the Eisenhower Doctrine and the formation of the dominoes theory, which exacerbated the Cold War. It remains to be seen how this strategy will play out[9].

---

[9] http://www.foreignpolicy.com/articles/2011/10/11/americas_pacific_century?page=full

This book examines some of the aspects of foreign and strategic policy discussed above in more detail, looking when appropriate into the history of US relations and exploring the real impact of US foreign policy, and of President Obama's particular contribution.

"Pakistan and not Iran[10] poses the imminent global nuclear threat."

---

[10]   http://abcnews.go.com/Politics/osama-bin-laden-dead-president-obama-full-remarks/story?id=13506069#.UDo2fkKhDFI

Chapter 1

US Foreign Policy in the Middle East

"The most striking outcome of the first Obama presidency has been a significant scaling up of the insecurity and instability in the Middle East."

In his first few months in office, President Obama was awarded the Nobel peace prize as a champion of dialogue, negotiations and nuclear disarmament. In 2011, he announced that the US would be accelerating the timetable for pullout from Iraq and then Afghanistan. He followed through on his promise when the US left Iraq later that year. The Arab Spring triggered hopes for a new era of democracy and prosperity in the Middle East, starting with Tunisia, Yemen, Egypt, Bahrain and Libya. Today, we have the evolving violence and civil war in Syria. Poised a few months before the elections and at a time when the global community and the US are facing critical decisions on what to do about Syria, it seems an opportune moment to review and study, the successes and challenges of the Obama Middle East strategy—has it worked or has it further destabilized a very tumultuous region, sowing the seeds for longer-term destabilization?

In examining this subject, I want to look at the main Arab countries involved in the the Islamic mosaic that defines allegiances and complexities in the Arab world and the Middle East, as well as, two important constants in the US relationship with the region: oil and the arms trade.

1

ISLAMIC MOSAIC: INTERWOVEN COMMUNITIES, INTERLOCKING HISTORIES

The countries of the Middle East form part of the mosaic of Islamic, Christian, Jewish and Orthodox communities that have determined the complex history of the region (*Map 1[11]*) and sown the seeds of many of the present day conflicts. The word "Arab" is used to apply to all these majority and minority inhabitants of the Middle East; the distinction of calling Jewish practitioners 'Israeli" only being drawn after the creation of Israel.

The term "Arab" masks significant and deep-rooted ideological differences between the Shiite and the Sunni going back to the fight for leadership of the early Islamic community between the Mecca-based followers of Abu Bakr, the anointed first Khalifa of Islam, and the followers of Hazrat[12] Ali, Hassan and Hussein in Baghdad. The Mecca-dwellers founded Sunni Islam and the Baghdad-dwellers branched off to lead the Shiites. Hazrat Hussein was martyred in a bid to take over the leadership of the Islamic community after the passing of Prophet Mohammed, setting the stage for the division of Islam. Centuries of violence and insurrection have led to a solid bedrock of grievances that fester to this day, barely below the surface in most Middle Eastern countries and in every Arabic heart.

---

[11]   http://gulf2000.columbia.edu/images/maps/Mid_East_Religion_lg.jpg

[12]   *Hazrat*is a Arab-Islamic word for prophet or saint.

MAP OF DISPERSION OF RELIGIONS AND RELIGIOUS SECTS IN THE MIDDLE EAST (MAP 1)

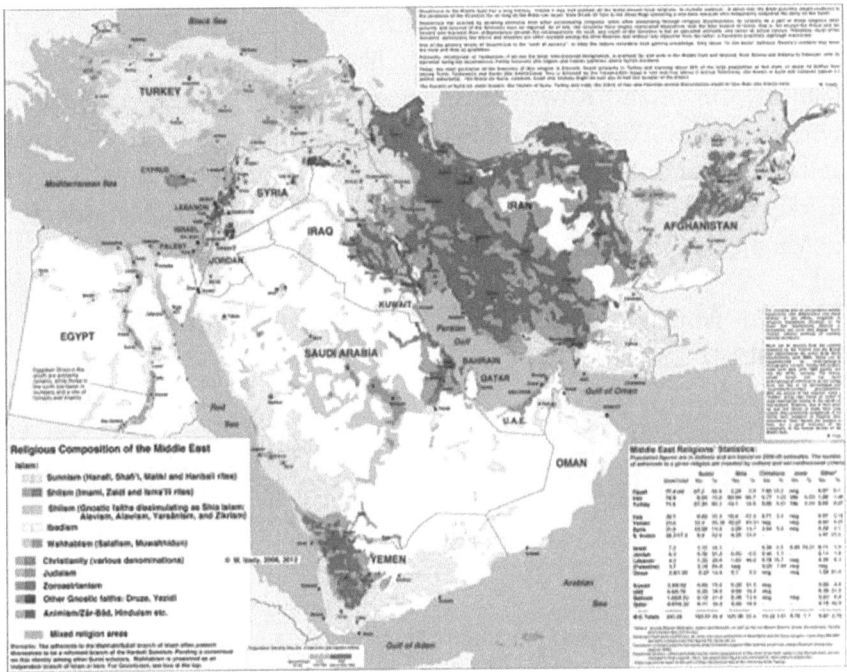

Oil: A major motivation of all US foreign policy and particularly of US strategy in the Middle East is continuous access to unlimited crude oil. For decades, this was the only motivation for US engagement in the region, until free trade became a significant component of the US-Middle East relations. The location of major oil deposits in the Middle East and the Arabian Gulf (*see Map 2[13]*) is interesting and pertinent to any political analysis of that region, as it highlights the fragility and vulnerability of major oil producing regions in countries like Saudi Arabia, where the population of main oil production areas are dominated by Shiite minorities.

US Defensive Deployments and Bases: The Middle East has had the highest number of US bases and deployed US military personnel (*see Map*

---

[13] h t t p : / / g u l f 2 0 0 0 . c o l u m b i a . e d u / i m a g e s / m a p s / MidEast_Religion_and_Oil_lg.jpg

3^{14}) after Europe for the last four decades. Defense relationships in the region constitute the main technical and training support to a majority of oil-rich Arab countries. In 2011 for example, the US trade totaled $66.3 billion, or 75 per cent, of global arms market, with Russia a distant runner-up at $4.8 billion. Countries like Saudi Arabia, UAE, Qatar, Bahrain, Oman and Kuwait have invested heavily in radar surveillance systems such as AWACS[15], and in advanced air force fighter jets, logistics and maintenance contracts. The US total of 44 per cent of the global arms market in 2010 rocketed to a staggering 79 per cent in 2011, mostly due to Middle East sales valued at some $56.3 billion that year[16].

MAP OF MIDDLE EAST OIL RESERVES AND RELIGIOUS COMMUNITIES (MAP 2)

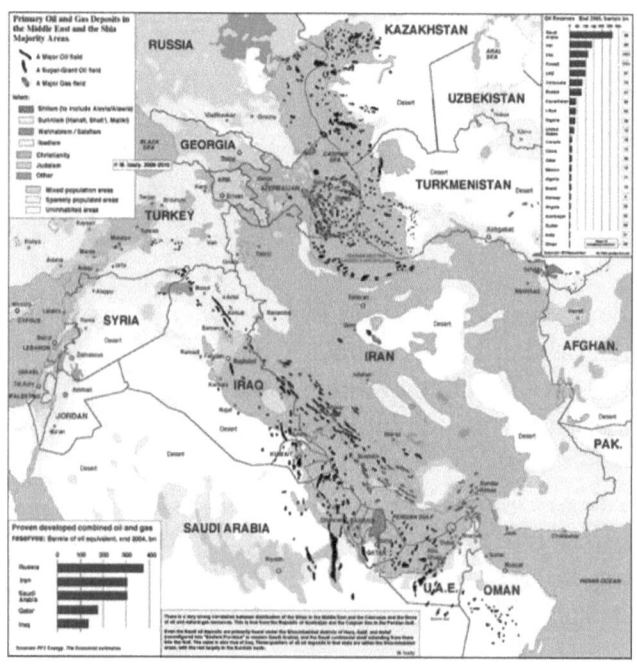

---

[14] http://gulf2000.columbia.edu/images/maps/ US bases in Middle East lg.jpg

[15] http://www.globalsecurity.org/military/world/gulf/rsaf.htm

[16] http://www.nytimes.com/2012/08/27/world/middleeast/us-foreign-arms-sales-reach-66-3-billion-in-2011.html? r=1&ref=todayspaper

MAP OF US DEPLOYMENTS AND US MILITARY BASES IN THE MIDDLE EAST (MAP 3)

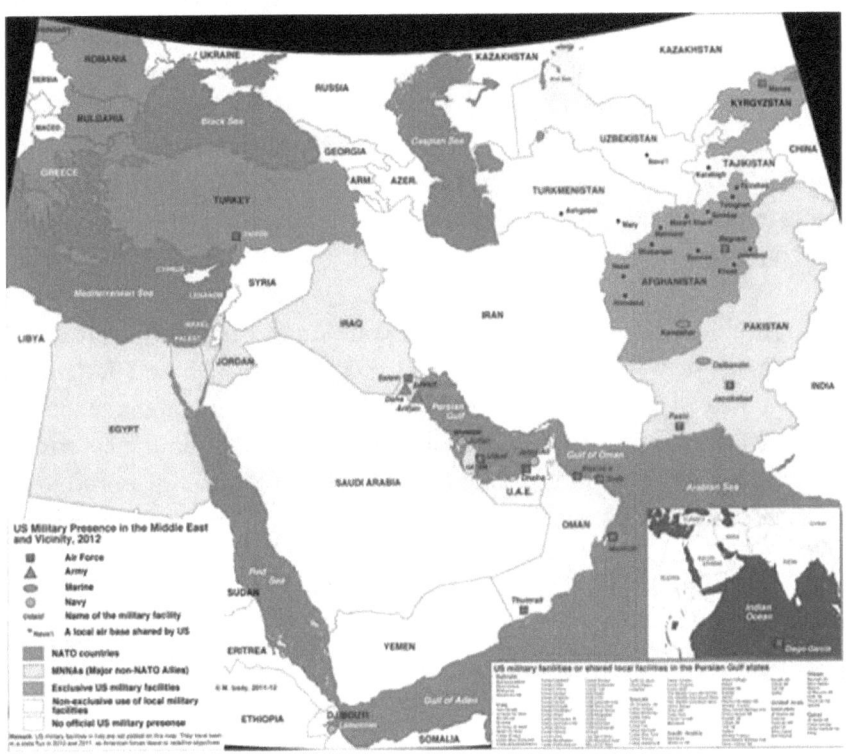

EGYPT

> *"Now the US has a choice. It can be reactive and brand President Mursi's administration an outlaw, or it can do what it has done since Mursi's election and refrain from comment . . . only critiquing human and civil rights violations by the State."*

The Arab Spring and it's amazing impact in Egypt has left long-time observers gasping for breath. In a few months of civil disobedience and peaceful protests, Egyptians overthrew decades of authoritarian rule. The US had brokered the Sinai Agreements[17], negotiating the deal through

---

[17] http://www.ibiblio.org/sullivan/docs/SinaiII.html

which Sadat signed the Camp David Accords with Israel. Sadat was assassinated soon afterwards, and following a brief power struggle, Hosni Mubarak took over, establishing a hegemonic dictatorship over Egypt. During his three decades of rule, the US flooded his government with aid money and military support estimated in the billions of dollars. Where this money ended up can only be conjectured, as very little trickled down to the Egyptian people. Accountability and transparency were not required, and the US does not appear to have forced Mubarak to consider democratization and political pluralism as a fundamental condition for the continuation of this assistance.

In short by doing nothing about the devolution of the political situation, the US *de facto* bankrolled the Mubarak dictatorship and its brutal control over all facets of Egypt. In return, the US was assured freedom of movement through the Suez Canal for global trade and commerce, and of the sanctity of the Sinai Agreement guaranteeing the stability and security of Israel's vital border with Egypt.

The ability of Muslim Brotherhood's President Mursi to maintain the Sinai Agreement as a sacrosanct cornerstone of Middle East peace, is essential for Egypt and Israel. President Mursi's recent moves to limit the power of the military and change its top leaders have alarmed analysts who recognize the pivotal role the Army plays in securing the Sinai. It is a priority for President Mursi to soothe the rising tide of Israeli concerns about, *inter alia,* the Sinai and the border with Palestine at Rafah. He needs to balance this in the coming months with the expectations and demands of his constituency and the Muslim Brotherhood.

Key Challenges: A month after taking office, President Mursi faces three main challenges. Due to the economic disruption caused by the revolution, one of the main sources of national revenue generation in Egypt, tourism, has all but dried up. Over a year of revolution has meant that the already below-living wages that a majority of Egyptians used to eke out of the tourist industry has diminished or completely disappeared. Simultaneously, inflation on basic food items such as meat, rice, beans and flour increased by 10.8 per cent as compared with just a year earlier[18], while hitherto robust government subsidies have evaporated. The Egyptian people are now expecting the new government to produce economic miracles. The downturn in tourism has hit every industry and commercial group in Egypt as shops and handicraft manufacturers need to absorb the double whammy of fewer tourists and their declining shopping budgets due to the global economic downturn.

The second immediate challenge for President Mursi is to develop the aura of credibility and reliability that he requires on the international and regional levels, and also on a personal level in Egypt with more liberal constituencies. The return of the tourist trade and the perception of his presidency in Europe, Middle East, Asia and the US has already been tarnished by his lack of appropriate response to the siege of the US Embassy in Cairo in September 2012—he gave contradictory messages and acted too slowly to reassure the US and other key partners of his ability to assume his responsibilities as the President of Egypt and a reliable international partner.

President Mursi's credibility will also impact the bilateral relationship with the US and Europe, hitherto key donors. Yet his recent moves to retire most of Egypt's military top brass, including Field Marshall Tentawi, has exacerbated concerns about the orientation of the President's nominations for their replacements[19]. The Egyptian Army remains a key guarantor of Egyptian security, not only in the Sinai and border with Palestine, but also potentially in maintaining security on borders with Libya and Sudan. His choice of army leaders would be critical in assuring seamless security in these important aspects, and more significantly, affects his credibility. The removal of trusted military personalities has also raised questions about the commitment of President Mursi to maintain Egypt's secular constitution and character.

---

[18] http://www.bloomberg.com/news/2012-05-10/egypt-s-april-inflation-slows-as-food-price-increases-ease-3-.html

[19] http://www.nytimes.com/2012/08/13/world/middleeast/egyptian-leader-ousts-military-chiefs.html?smid=pl-share

President Mursi's third challenge is to re-assert the supremacy of rule of law and control rampant corruption and nepotism in the Egyptian civil service and security forces.

The US-Egypt Relationship

"If the (Iran-Syria) proposed mediation comes to pass and is a success, Egypt will have conclusively ended Iran's isolation in the region."

A decades-long relationship has been put in question by the election of President Mursi.

He is aligned with the Muslim Brotherhood, which remains a blacklisted outlaw organization in the eyes of the US State Department. US contributions to Egypt have been significant in financial and military terms, while the price paid for this support and for keeping the Sinai physically within Egypt was three decades of political suppression, dictatorship and strong police/military control and harassment at the hands of President Hosni Mubarak. In a few weeks since coming to power, President Mursi has already challenged the *status quo* within Egypt by changing the entire military leadership, with whom the US and all other interlocutors had established relationships. In appointing young military officers he trusts but are relatively unknown to the US, to these high-ranking positions, Mursi has set a high bar of independence of decision and action, perhaps to become a hallmark of his presidential style.

The second manifestation of the autonomous line of the Mursi presidency emerged during his first big international appearance, when President Mursi proposed an Egyptian-brokered regional mediation of the Syrian conflict, bringing together Saudi Arabia and Turkey (supporters of the Syrian opposition forces) and Iran, the key supporter of the Assad government[20]. By so doing, Mursi is delivering to the Egyptian people on his promise to return Egypt to a global international politic befitting a great nation. How the US will react to this initiative, bringing together the key regional actors implicated in the Syrian conflict, but without any role

---

[20] http://www.nytimes.com/2012/08/27/world/middleeast/egyptian-president-seeks-regional-initiative-for-syria-peace.html?ref=todayspaper

for the US, remains to be seen. The inclusion of Iran, while acknowledged by Saudi Arabia, continues to be controversial in the US and Israel that both perceive the Egyptian proposal with suspicion and irritation. If the proposed mediation comes to pass and is a success, Egypt will have conclusively ended Iran's isolation in the region.

Mursi has now signaled the advent of a new regional actor in the Middle East and also indicated that as President of Egypt, he will not hesitate to declare and follow, an independent line in Egyptian foreign and regional policy. It is also important how Israel will react to and perceive Mursi's decision firstly to attend the Non-Align Summit in Tehran and secondly, Mursi's new mediation offer. Israel will probably feel rising hysteria as it sees a big neighbor and a key security partner in the region moving to neutralize Egyptian relations with Iran by visiting that country and including them in a key negotiation initiative.

The US record in Egypt has been replete with mistakes, and carries a legacy of supporting a dictatorial status quo without promoting the evolution over decades of a democratic and pluralistic society. Now the US has a choice. It can be reactive and brand President Mursi's administration an outlaw, or it can do what it has done since Mursi's election and refrain from comment. The only positive approach from the Obama administration is to allow Mursi to fully show his hand, only critiquing human and civil rights violations by the State.

A positive sign emerged in early September 2012, when the US announced final negotiations on a $1 billion debt relief package, a third of Egypt's total debt to the US. The Obama government also offered $345 million finance and loan guarantees for US companies investing in Egypt and a $60 million[21] investment fund for Egyptians to start new enterprises. President Mursi has also requested a $4.8 billion loan from the IMF to bridge a serious budget gap and a steep fall in currency reserves. Measures

---

[21]   http://blogs.voanews.com/breaking-news/2012/09/04/us-nears-deal-for-1-billion-in-egypt-debt-relief/
http://www.nytimes.com/2012/09/05/opinion/egypts-economic-struggle.html

such as these are critical in neutralizing the relationship and refocusing on future collaborative strategies.

Strengthening the US-Egypt relationship in the Mursi era necessitates President Obama's personal decision and involvement on how to approach Egypt's nascent effort on Syria, which might allow Egypt to become a valuable and trusted centrist interlocutor in the Middle East.

SAUDI ARABIA

> *"The US total of 44 per cent of the global arms market in 2010 rocketed to a staggering 79 per cent in 2011, mostly due to Middle East sales valued at some $56.3 billion that year."*

Britain and the United States are Saudi Arabia's longest and most solid supporters. The present Al-Saud family took over control of a loose conglomeration of tribes and lands between WWI and WWII. The US relationship is based on two connected streams: Saudi supply of unlimited crude oil, and deep security cooperation between the US and Saudi Arabia.

This cooperation escalated in the aftermath of the Iranian revolution in 1979. Saudi Arabia became the staging post and base for US military operations all over the Middle East and Arabian Gulf, particularly in response to the December 1979 Soviet invasion of Afghanistan. These two separate but consecutive events placed the spotlight on Saudi Arabia's strategic location at the heart of the Arabian Gulf, its relatively sparse and docile population and the willingness of its leaders to be completely co-opted by US foreign policy priorities. Pakistan, then a close ally of both the US and Saudi Arabia, joined them in establishing a bulwark of resistance against the Soviet expansionism and against the spillover of Shiite nationalism from Iran.

The US strengthened its security rapport with Saudi Arabia (*see information in the Introductory chapter and Map 3, page 5*), as a source of high value and critical military and air force equipment, and also providing essential training, maintenance and re-supply contracts. Secondly, the US built key military bases in Saudi Arabia, which provide it with guaranteed and unfettered access in the region, and allow it to carry out sensitive intelligence operations. Due to the domination of this relationship by the US, it is probable that Saudi Arabia will replace Pakistan as a center for drone warfare if, as anticipated, Pakistan starts to shut down its strategic security relationship with the US (*see section on Pakistan on page 38*).

Challenges: Saudi Arabia faces its own challenges. Significant Shiite indigenous populations inhabit the oil-rich regions to the southwest of the country (*see Map 1, page 3*). But the percentage of national investment and development returning to these minority areas and populations is very unfavorable, giving rise to discrete but definite grievances. Security concerns surfaced when Shiite majority populations in Bahrain started their quest for increased representation and democratization, anticipating that political mobilization might spillover into Saudi Arabia. However, Saudi Arabia's draconian and omnipresent police force made sure that suspect populations were adequately warned of corrective action should they choose to follow their brethren's path of resistance.

> *"The apparent opening of Saudi Arabia and the Gulf Arabs to China could be a game changer for the foreign policy of the region, and have far-reaching impact on the Arab relationship with the USA and Europe, if it materializes on the coming months."*

More significant is the challenge posed to the established leadership by the high number of Saudi-born Islamic Jihadists and fundamentalists, such as Osama Bin Laden himself. The roots of this development lie in the rise of fundamentalist Wahhabism within Saudi Arabia, coupled with the joint Saudi-US decision in the 1970s and 1980s to finance Jihadist resistance to Soviet domination in Afghanistan via Pakistan. A US strategy to strengthen the resistance movements in Afghanistan identified Pakistan as the optimal location for training camps and indoctrination centers, sometimes financed directly by the US and sometimes through their most valued surrogate in the region, Saudi Arabia. The role of Saudi Arabia in the jihadisation of both Pakistan and Afghanistan is significant, and draws from Saudi Arabia's stated foreign policy priority of promoting Sunni Wahhabi Islam globally and re-introducing Sharia law in the Islamic world[22].

As a US surrogate in the region, Saudi Arabia has used its network to finance local-level agitators and insurgent groups, as an example, in Syria. It has supported the implementation of US Middle East strategy, often inciting violent conflict in neighboring states (*see Syria, page 29*) and states such as Iran that are out of favor with the US.

Yet Saudi Arabia has had a free hand in managing its own complex nation, with almost complete exemption from US conditionalities on observing international and established human rights laws. Saudi Arabia is a corrupt dictatorship of oppressors that give virtually no freedom of speech, religion, movement or assembly to their people. Women live as chattel in what amounts to human bondage and are not allowed to drive or travel without the accompaniment of a responsible male relative.

More Recent Developments in Saudi Foreign Policy

China: After decades of disunity and prevarication, the Gulf Arabs and Saudi Arabia seem to suddenly have achieved policy cohesion in the face of a potentially nuclear-capable Iran.

The first evidence of this change was the welcome reception, including lucrative oil and trade deals that Gulf Arab states offered Chinese Prime Minister Wen Jiaobao on his visit in early 2012, to the Gulf and Saudi Arabia. The Arabs offer oil supply deals that would replace and *defacto* eliminate China's reliance on Iranian oil. (China depends on Iran for nearly one-third of its total imported oil supply). In exchange they ask for cooperation with the West on sanctions and trade embargoes aimed at containing the Iranian nuclear program, a subject on which China remains intransigent in terms of policy.

---

[22]   http://www.asecondlookatthesaudis.com/sitebuildercontent/sitebuilderfiles/
asecondlookatthesaudisaglobalagenda.pdf
http://thegreatchessboard.wordpress.com/tag/jihad/
http://www.nysun.com/foreign/saudi-royals-mask-a-jihad-agenda/52999/

For China, this visit has marked a huge change in the quality and content of the relationship with Saudi Arabia and the Gulf Arabs, who traditionally have been singularly focused on their cooperation and trade with the US. This sudden potential for upgrading the Chinese-Arab relationship is something that China has cherished as a long-term objective, in addition to maintaining its relationship with Iran. The apparent opening of Saudi Arabia and the Gulf Arabs to China could be a game changer for the foreign policy of the region, and have far-reaching impact on the Arab relationship with the USA and Europe, if it materializes on the coming months.

Bahrain: In 2010, a secularist Bahraini civil society movement started peaceful protests for increased political representation and democratization. Saudi Arabia was quick to come to the assistance of the Emir of Bahrain. It sent in trained Saudi police units to support local Bahraini police in violently subduing the peaceful movement, causing significant civilian deaths and millions of dollars of collateral damage. In May 2012, after a green light from the US State Department, Saudi Arabia and Bahrain entered discussions aimed at exploring the coming together of the two nations in a "political union"[23]. The case of Bahrain is complicated. It is rooted in an 100-year-old movement for increased political and civil rights (*see Case Study: Bahrain, next section*), which will not vanish in the event of a political union.

CASE STUDY: BAHRAIN

> *". . . throughout the violent, often fatal repression by the Bahraini leadership and their security apparatus of the long-standing, peacefully secular movement for increased diplomacy and political representation, the US never imposed conditionalities of human rights, human dignity and political freedoms that have been used as justification to penalize so many other countries and leaderships."*

---

[23] http://www.independent.co.uk/news/world/middle-east/gulf-keeps-close-watch-as-saudis-hold-union-talks-with-bahrain-7746869.html
http://www.independent.co.uk/news/world/middle-east/deal-with-saudis-to-shore-up-bahrains-repressive-regime-7743529.html

A History of Bahrain: The Rule of The British and Al-Khalifa[24]

The saga of the Al-Khalifa family, the present Emir of Bahrain, begins in 1783 when the family moved to Bahrain's Jaww region from Kuwait and later-day Iraq. In 1820, the Al Khalifa tribe regained power in Bahrain and entered into a treaty[25] relationship with Great Britian, the later being the dominant military power in the Persian Gulf, as it was then called. This treaty recognized the Al Khalifa as the rulers ("Al-Hakim" in Arabic) of Bahrain. It was the first of several treaties including the 1861 Perpetual Treaty of Peace and Friendship[26], further revised in 1892 and 1951. This treaty was similar to those entered into by the British Government with the other Persian Gulf principalities. It specified that the ruler could not dispose of any of his territory except to the United Kingdom and could not enter into relationships with any foreign government without British consent. In return the British promised to protect Bahrain from all aggression by sea and to lend support in case of land attack. More importantly, the British promised to support the rule of the Al Khalifa in Bahrain, securing its unstable position as rulers of the country.

In 1860, the Government of Al Khalifa negotiated terms of protection with the Ottoman Wali of Baghdad for protection against the British when they tried to colonize Bahrain. Finally, in a last attempt to resist formal British colonization, Sheikh Al-Khalifa requested military assistance from Iran, but the Government of Iran at that time provided no aid to protect Bahrain from British aggression. As a result the Government of British India eventually overpowered Bahrain, replacing the Sheikh with his brother Sheikh Ali as Ruler under British rule and protection. In 1868, Britian and Al Khalifa rulers signed another agreement making Bahrain part of the British protectorate territories in the Persian Gulf. It specified that the ruler could not dispose of any of his territory except to the United Kingdom and could not enter into relationships with any foreign government without British consent. In return the British promised to protect Bahrain from all aggression by sea and to lend support in case of

---

24   http://en.wikipedia.org/wiki/History_of_Bahrain#Treaties_with_Britain

25   http://en.wikipedia.org/wiki/General_Maritime_Treaty_of_1820

26   http://en.wikipedia.org/wiki/Perpetual_Truce_of_Peace_and_Friendship

land attack. More importantly the British promised to support the rule of the Al Khalifa in Bahrain, securing its unstable position as rulers of the country. Other agreements in 1880 and 1892 sealed the protectorate status of Bahrain to the British. This bought peace and trade, and a new prosperity.

British Occupation: Unrest amongst the people of Bahrain began when Britain officially established complete dominance over the territory in 1892. The first revolt and widespread uprising took place in March 1895 against Sheikh Issa bin Ali, then ruler of Bahrain. Sheikh Issa was the first of the Al Khalifa to rule without Iranian relations. The uprising developed further with some protesters killed by British forces.

As a result, Bahrain underwent a period of major social reform between 1926 and 1957, supported by the British and led by Sheikh Hamad Ibn Isa Al-Khalifa (1872-1942) The country's first modern school was established in 1919, with the opening of the Al-Hiddaya Boys School, while the Persian Gulf's first girls school opened in 1928. British power was consolidated when they removed the Ruler in 1923 and replaced him with his son. They also banished and exiled key opposition groups resisting modernization and reforms.

The discovery of oil in 1932 by the Bahrain Petroleum Company[27] brought rapid modernization to Bahrain and in 1935 the British moved its entire Middle Eastern command from Iran to Bahrain. British influence continued to grow as the country developed, culminating in an appointment of a *defacto* Governor to parallel the rule of the Al-Khalifa. After World War II, increasing anti-British sentiment spread throughout the Arab World and led to riots in Bahrain. The riots were led by the Jewish community, which included distinguished writers, singers, accountants, engineers and middle managers working for the oil company, textile merchants with business all over the peninsula, and other free professionals.

The National Union Committee (NUC), a leftist nationalist movement associated with the labour unions, was formed in 1954 calling for the end of British interference and for comprehensive political reforms. After 1956

---

[27] http://en.wikipedia.org/wiki/Bahrain_Petroleum_Company

Suez Canal war during which NUC supported Egyptian nationalists, the British decided to put an end to the NUC challenge to their presence in Bahrain. The NUC and its offshoots were declared illegal. Its leaders were arrested, tried and imprisoned. Some fled the country while others were forcibly deported. Strikes and riots continued during the 1960s and in March 1965, an uprising resulted in the laying off of hundreds of Bahraini workers at the Bahrain Petroleum Company. Several people died in the violent clashes between protesters and police.

Finally in 1968, when the British Government announced its decision to end the treaty relationships with the Persian Gulf sheikdoms, Bahrain joined together with Qatar and seven other small Sheikhdoms in the United Arab Emirates. By mid-1971, however, the nine sheikhdoms still had not agreed on the terms of union. Accordingly, Bahrain sought independence as a separate entity becoming formally independent as the State of Bahrain on December 16, 1971. At independence, the permanent Royal Navy presence in Bahrain ended and the United States Navy moved onto the 10 acres (40,000 m²) previously occupied by British operations. The installation later grew into the headquarters for the US Fifth Fleet[28].

A new National Assembly was elected in 1973, and a new constitution was approved in 1973 that included some controversial provisions that the Sheikh could not agree on. Having used emergency powers contained in the new constitution, the Sheikh suspended and dismissed the entire National Assembly and enforced by decree, the controversial State Security Law. This commenced the modern era of political agitation for Bahrainis against their ruling family.

Oil Money Consolidates Dictatorship

The Kingdom emerged just as the price of oil skyrocketed as part of the OPEC oil rises after the Arab-Israeli war of 1973, while Bahrain's own reserves were being depleted the high oil price meant there was massive capitalization in the Kingdom's neighbors. The Kingdom was able to exploit the opportunities arising from the Lebanese Civil War starting in 1975. Bahrain offered a new location at the center of the booming Persian

---

[28]   http://en.wikipedia.org/wiki/United_States_Fifth_Fleet

Gulf banking industry, offering a large educated indigenous workforce and sound fiscal regulations, thereby cashing in on the opportunity to become a regional financial center.

This bolstered the development of the middle class and gives Bahrain a very different class structure from its tribal dominated neighbors. Although there had long been a large Indian presence in Bahrain, it was at this time that mass migration to the Kingdom began to take off. The consequences for the Kingdom's demographics, were large numbers of immigrants from countries such as Pakistan, Egypt and Iran, attracted by better salaries than at home.

Continuing Political Struggle for Democracy

The 1979 Iranian Revolution had a huge impact on the political aspirations of the significant Shiite majority in Bahrain and on the underground NUC movement as a rejection of UK and US domination. Years of political stasis, the collapse of the price of oil and growing frustration at the lack of democracy exploded in an uprising in 1994. There was also a strong sense of grievance due to perceived discrimination against the majority Shiite population of Bahrain by the Al Khalifa rulers. Joint Shiite and Sunni initiatives aimed at restoration of the National Assembly and the constitution of 1975 were rebuffed violently by State security forces, with mass arrests, torture and harassment.

In 1999, the incoming Sheikh Hamad tried to end the political repression that had defined the 1990s by scrapping security laws, releasing all political prisoners, instituting elections, giving women the vote and promising a return to constitutional rule. The move brought an end to political violence, but did not initially bring about reconciliation between the government and most of the opposition groups, because the changes were seen as largely superficial, failing to address the plethora of deep-rooted aspirations of the Bahraini people in the new millennium.

Unceasing Demands for Democratization: On 14 February 2011, the protests in Bahrain started again, initially aimed at achieving greater political freedom and respect for human rights; they were not intended to directly threaten the monarchy. Lingering frustration among the Shiite majority with Sunni rule was a major root cause, although the protests in Tunisia and Egypt are cited as the inspiration for the demonstrations. During February and March 2011, as many as 150,000 people turned out to protest their abridged political rights in the city center of Bahrain. Government crack down was ruthless and swift. King Hamad declared a three-month state of emergency on 15 March 2011[29].

The police response has been described as a "brutal" crackdown on peaceful and unarmed protestors, including doctors, bankers and businessmen. The police carried out midnight house raids in Shiite neighborhoods, beatings at checkpoints, and denial of medical care in a "campaign of intimidation". More than 2,929 people have been arrested, and at least five people died due to torture while in police custody. On 23 November 2011 the Bahrain Independent Commission of Inquiry[30] released its report on its investigation of the events, finding that the government had systematically tortured prisoners and committed other human rights violations. The Bahraini government has refused entry to several international human rights groups, UN inspectors and news organizations, while over 80 people were killed as a result of state orchestrated violence.

US-Bahraini Relations

> *"Happening on President Obama's watch, the US appears to have been unable to moderate the national leadership of Bahrain, their client state, in its disproportionate use of force against its civilian unarmed population."*

The US took over British military bases in Bahrain in 1971 after independence, and in 1991 signed a defense pact making it the home of the US Fifth Fleet. In 2004, the US signed a Free Trade Agreement with Bahrain. Since 9/11, along with Saudi Arabia, the US presence in Bahrain has been a cornerstone of US strategic security policy in the Arabian Gulf, particularly vis-à-vis Iran. This is the reason that throughout the violent, often fatal repression by the Bahraini leadership and their

---

29 http://en.wikipedia.org/wiki/State_of_emergency
30 http://en.wikipedia.org/wiki/Bahrain_Independent_Commission_of_Inquiry

security apparatus of the long-standing, peacefully secular movement for increased diplomacy and political representation, the US never imposed conditionalities of human rights, human dignity and political freedoms that have been used as justification to penalize so many other countries and leaderships.

The duplicity of US foreign policy towards Bahrain was further revealed on 11 May 2012, as the State Department announced that the US would be resuming scheduled arms supplies to Bahrain and its violent leadership[31]. This step followed Saudi Arabian deployment of trained police and military units to help the Bahraini Sheikhs maintain law and order. Approximately 3000 civilians have been arrested and at least 5 of these unarmed civilians have died from torture while in detention[32]. Doctors giving life saving medical care to civilians injured during sectarian violence were attacked, arrested and prevented from giving any medical care, and medical facilities were destroyed. Indiscriminate, continuous and excessive use of tear gas[33] has raised fears as well as official protests from international human rights organizations, who note that prolonged and excessive exposure to tear gas as is the case in Bahrain amounts to killing and poisoning civilian unarmed populations by chemical warfare[34]. A significant part of this tear gas is supplied by the US.

Happening on President Obama's watch, the US appears to have been unable to moderate the national leadership of Bahrain, their client state, in its disproportionate use of force against its civilian unarmed population. A further question arises why the International Criminal Court and International Court of Justice have not legally cautioned the Emir and his government on the excessive use of force.

---

[31] http://security.blogs.cnn.com/2012/05/11/u-s-resumes-arms-sales-to-bahrain/

[32] http://en.wikipedia.org/wiki/Bahraini_uprising_(2011-present)

[33] http://www.nytimes.com/2012/08/01/world/middleeast/bahrain-criticized-for-torrent-of-tear-gas-use.html

[34] http://physiciansforhumanrights.org/press/press-releases/bahrain-uses-tear-gas-as-lethal-weapon.html

Currently a majority but not all of the population associated with the uprising are Shiites, another manifestation of the Islamic mosaic and inherited from Bahrain's colorful history. This simple fact may explain the deficits of justice in the treatment of the Arab Spring in Bahrain by the US and other democracy champions in Europe. The implication would be that the US, and President Obama directly, are not enforcing high human rights and democratization standards to Bahrain because the restive victim population is Shiite.

Conclusion: Onwards Bahrain

The failure of the US, during President Obama's watch, to mentor corrective action and stop supporting the indiscriminate killing, injuring and poisoning of Bahraini civilians is an indictment of the Obama Administration and foreign and strategic policy in the Middle East itself. Continued lack of rectification further condemns President Obama on his lack of perspective on the long roots and depth of commitment of the Bahraini Arab Spring. The Bahraini revolution will continue to try and change the system of corruption enforced by its Sheikh leaders. As the next section should demonstrate, in both the case of Iran and of Bahrain, resident Obama has squandered opportunities and left key policy goals abstract and unrealized.

IRAN

> *"If Iran ever intended to open its nuclear program for inspection, the lack of confidence created by US' cyber warfare initiative conclusively put an end to it, further convincing the Iranian leadership of the malevolence of the P5+1 and the US in particular."*

The Iranian saga really started in 1951, with the *Abandan Crisis*. Prime Minister Mohammed Mossadeq initiated a program of nationalization of the Anglo-Iranian Oil Company (AIOC). This move came after years of popular dissention at the lack of transparency in financial management and in the sharing of profits. Britain owned a 85 per cent share of all proceedings and income, and Iran itself was left with 15 per cent. In 1951, the Iranian Parliament approved the nationalization of what was at the time the largest and most lucrative business holding of the British Empire.

While the US, led at the time by President Truman, was publically advising Britain to moderate its response, the US Embassy in Tehran cooperated covertly with the British secret service to plot and stage a coup against Prime Minister Mossadeq. In the spring of 1953, the first coup mounted by the US and Britain failed. But the second coup, *Operation Ajax*, succeeded in installing Mohammed Reza Pahalvi at the top of leadership as the "Shah of Iran"[35].

Following the coup, the US provided billions of dollars of financial and military assistance to Iran. Very little, however, seeped down to the Iranian people in terms of health, education or civil benefits. Successive US Presidents and administrations never demanded accountability from the Shah and never applied any pressure on him to liberalize his security stranglehold on the people of Iran and institute democratic reform. The seeds of distrust and dislike and the impression that the US and Britain, in particular, were raping Iran's natural and oil resources to the detriment of the people of Iran were firmly planted in the minds and understanding of the nation.

Counter-coup: The lid finally blew off the extremely corrupt and cruel regime of the Shah when the people of Iran mounted a revolution in 1979. The US was caught wrong-footed in the country after intelligence reports had deduced as late as early 1979 that Iran was stable and not under any immediate threat of revolution. To an extent, after decades of direct and open support of the dictatorship of Reza Pahalvi, it was too late for the US to salvage the relationship.

On 4 November 1979, angered by the refugee status granted to the Shah by the US, the revolutionary Muslim Student's Followers of the Imam's Line invaded the US embassy and held 52 US diplomatic hostages for 444 days. Frustrated with the inability to negotiate with the Revolution, on 7 April 1980 the US broke off diplomatic relations. These have yet to be restored. On 24 April 1980, in what became know as *Operation Eagle Claw*, the US mounted a failed mission to rescue the hostages. Eight US military service men lost their lives in the effort which failed.

---

[35] http://en.wikipedia.org/wiki/Iran—United States relations#1977. E2.80.931979: Carter administration

Alliance with Saddam Hussein in the Iran-Iraq war, the Iran-Contra Affair and a series of other backhanded US initiatives against Iran, including a 1988 attack against Iranian owned and operated oil rigs in the Arabian Gulf, coffined the US-Iran relationship. Today, this relationship is so damaged that re-establishing trust and credibility of the US in this relationship looks as challenging as Iran trying to convince the P5+1 (US, UK, France, Russia, China and Germany) negotiators that its nuclear agenda is an energy issue. Added to the mix is revolutionary Iran's dismal record of allowing political opposition parties and leaders to peacefully practice their universal right to representation. In the 2012 Presidential election, a fair vote was deemed impossible by international human rights organizations[36]. After the election, Mir Hussein Moussavi, the leaders of the Green opposition party, and others have been under virtual house arrest.

Despite all these challenges, President Obama had a unique and historic opportunity to transform this relationship during his first term. One of the promises of Obama's election campaign was to change the course of the US-Iran relationship. In the first year or so, he tentatively tried to reframe the conversation with Iran. But the gambit amounted to a superficial foray. He did not take the time to really analyze and open a dialogue with Iran.

Transformation of this complex relationship would need dedicated and intensive demonstrations of goodwill and the slow re-building of confidence in an atmosphere without aggressive policies such as cyber warfare. This has not come to pass. While President Obama has upheld negotiations as the better alternative to the nuclear debacle in Iran[37], there is little likelihood that he will be able to muster enough credibility and confidence among the Iranians. With cyber warfare and other covert initiatives commenced against Iran, President Obama seems to have continued the script of the 1953 Mossadeq coup and direct support for the dictatorship of the Shah in following a devious and covert agenda of warfare against Iran.

---

[36] http://www.hrw.org/news/2012/03/01/iran-fair-vote-impossible

[37] http://www.foreignaffairs.com/articles/137731/kenneth-n-waltz/why-iran-should-get-the-bomb

There is a lot at stake in the continuing nuclear discussions between Iran and the P5+1. Through the testimony of history charted in this book, not to mention the huge body of knowledge and scholarship on the temerity and resilience of the Iranian people, and their ability to sacrifice for their state and their religion, the impression is given that it will not be easy to vanquish Iran easily or without significant resistance.

The continuing paralysis of the US-Iran "non-relationship" has been exacerbated by the fact that Obama himself did not take the lead in this critical policy initiative. By not adopting a deeper policy orientation, President Obama early on condemned the US discourse with Iran to remain conflictive and contentious. When it came to nuclear negotiations, transformation and deal making, this sensitive arena could not jump out of the relationship "box". While negotiation is the best alternative to an enlarged regional war if a military option is used in Iran, the balance of the eventual policy option that will be adopted will depend on the extent to which the Obama administration, or the next incumbent President, is able to control Israeli trigger-happiness and infuse a modicum of stability in the US-Iran relations. Signs are already emerging that President Obama is leaning this way[38]. President Obama may yet be credited with taking the decision to lead the world to safety, over triggering a larger Israel-Iran conflict in the Middle East.

CAMEO ANALYSIS: A CASE FOR COOPERATION BETWEEN IRAN AND ISRAEL

Perversely, Iran and Israel are very much alike. Their peoples have a long history, shaped by common heritage and civilizations that shaped the very evolution of world history and culture. They now are locked in a struggle that could destroy what they have been bequeathed. Both Iran and Israel are isolated and embattled in their regional settings, building military supremacy and nuclear capacity to create deterrence, security and protection for their countries. Their quest for national resurgence and the uniqueness of their peoples (both Jews and Persians have unique language and history that identifies them as a people) have contributed to their

---

[38]   http://www.algemeiner.com/2012/09/03/talk-on-iran-'red-lines'-comes-after-u-s-general-distances-himself-from-israeli-strike/

current rogue political status in the international community. Both are militarily powerful and to be respected for the damage they can inflict, potentially at the global level. Both Israel and Iran are accused of covertly building up nuclear war capacity, and Israel is assumed to already possess nuclear powered warheads. They are both religious national collectives: Israel the homeland of the Jews, and Iran the homeland of the Shiite Muslims. Their people have a concentration of talent in creativity, art and business. In another world, Israel and Iran might have more in common then in opposition.

Israel has an advantage that Iran forfeited when they revolted against the US—backed Shah Pahlavi in the Iranian revolution of 1979: US support. Israel also has an advantage in being historically perceived as a victim nation after the horrific WWII holocaust, and has enjoyed special protection and privileged technological, military and economic relationships with a number of European countries and the US. Iran in the mean time has had to rely on its natural energy resources and its own industry to float its growing economy and country. Despite the challenges, Iran has developed impressive networks of global economic partnerships and trade, overcoming the financial and economic isolation that is the objective of the US-led sanctions regimes.

Israel has an impressive economic record, but at the global economic level it's partnerships have been preceded by diplomatic and economic facilitation on its behalf by the US. Israeli partnership with Turkey, for example, was a direct by-product of US policy objectives and not a natural evolution. Israel finds it relatively harder than Iran to move in the international arena, as many countries still perceive it as a pariah on the Palestinian question.

Iran, on the other hand, is secretly admired by many for its "chutzpah" in striking an independent posture against the US. Observers including myself expected Iran to rise above the zero-sum policy game it is playing against the US, to a more pragmatic global diplomacy. Such a move was preempted by the initiation of covert cyber warfare by President Obama, in what amounted to a signal to the Iranians that US strategy vis-à-vis Iran was not going to change in the short run.

ISRAEL

> *"President Obama may yet be credited with taking the decision to lead the world to safety, over triggering a larger Israel-Iran conflict in the Middle East."*

Israel is the USA's most important political and strategic partner, and has been for the last four decades. The common belief is that Israel and the Jewish lobby in the United States control a number of important financial, political and foreign policy processes and outcomes. This is because of an inexplicably close relationship between the US and Israel in a multitude of arenas, as well as in strategic security policy, particularly in the Middle East. So strong is this relationship that it is perceived as determining US policy and actions towards individual states in the Middle and Near East.

Over the decades, this relationship has been blamed for the genesis and causality for many seemingly "unfair" policies applied towards the Arabs, and a significant collective trauma surrounds the Arab perception that Israel's success is at the cost of the unmaking of the Arabs, thousands of lives and the very existence of Palestine. Be this as it may, three aspects of this relationship shed light on the complex yet elementary bilateral relations between the two countries and on who is leading and to what extent.

Economy: Over the last two or three decades, Israel has evolved as an oasis of commercial success and prosperity for those that are considered full citizens. The capsule miracle that is Israel started with a diaspora of Jews that took refuge from a multitude of homelands all over the globe. They brought with them their home cultures, crafts, habits and skills, strengths that the new Israel wove together with commercial savvy. It capitalized on diaspora networks to draw resources, business and opportunities to its growing economy.

One example of the Israeli economic miracle is the diamond cutting and processing industry. Faced with competition from established diamond centers like Antwerp, and emerging centers such as Mumbai and Chennai in India, Israeli commercial networks[39] drew on their technical expertise and historic expertise to tap a huge global market. They have overtaken Antwerp as a diamond hub in terms of volume of trade.

In part, the new market niche was created because they have remained active in main diamond producing countries such as the Democratic Republic of the Congo, Namibia, South Africa and others, routing supply directly to Israel regardless of the imposition of trade sanctions and other restrictions. Secondly, a vast number of Antwerp companies were partially or wholly owned by Jewish interests that established parallel sub-offices in Israel, over time shifting the volume of cutting and processing business to their Israel affiliate. This left in place a selling market in Antwerp, but bumped up and expanded the lucrative cutting and processing sectors in Israel significantly. It also provided a politically legitimate business cover to Israeli products that might otherwise have met with resistance from the largest markets and buyers. This combination of pragmatic yet traditional market creation and expansion has characterized the format for Israeli commerce, supported to a large extent by US-based and Jewish-American businesses.

Military-Industrial Complex: The most significant collaboration between the US and Israel has been in the area of military, security and intelligence capacity building and the creation of an Israeli military-industrial complex. In the 1960's and 1970's, Israel benefitted from CIA and Pentagon assistance to train, equip and deploy its small but highly effective security forces. Apart from political support, security and intelligence capacity building are the most significant contributions that the US has made to Israel. The building up of Israeli research and production capacity in military hardware and intelligence or spy software means that Israel today has some of the most sophisticated production of intelligence and military spyware in the world. This industry was heavily supported by the US.

After it came online linked to private sector security companies in the US, the Israeli military-industrial complex commenced supplying a number of informal clients globally—those that the US did not want

---

39 http://www.bloomberg.com/news/2010-05-31/israeli-s-diamonds-are-dubai-s-best-friend-as-profit-trumps-emirate-policy.html

to have directly linked to its own foreign policy positions. This informal sector cooperation has grown[40] as countries such as Turkey, Malaysia and Indonesia have purchased and invested in Israeli manufactured equipment and technology with maintenance and follow-up contracts through US or European affiliates. There are derivative industries, particularly in R&D for chemical and biological spheres that are also thriving, but difficult to trace and research because of information blackout.

As one of his first initiatives, President Obama sold Israel the short-range missiles protection system *Iron Dome*. In July 2012, in response to increasing insecurity from its southern Sinai flank, Israel requested and President Obama approved an additional US$70 million extension to the *Iron Dom program*[41]. This constitutes the single largest and most significant military commitment to Israel from the US over the last decade, and underscores President Obama's commitment to Israel security as a US priority.

Foreign and Security Policy: Israel and the US are linked inextricably in the assessment, formulation and execution of foreign and security policy. Over decades this collaboration has deepened, although sometimes appearing to become unbalanced in favor of one or the other.

The truth is that Israel has always been shielded and protected by a major external power. Right after its creation, it was the UK until WWII, after which Israel worked hard to establish a deeper relationship with the US. Their initial objective was to gain US patronage and protection against aggressive pro-Palestinian agendas and a hostile "neighborhood". Over the next five or six decades, Israel has thrived under US protection. Even financial support from US-based Jews was essential in sustaining their economic build-up. The Israeli weapons industry and their nuclear capacity has totally been developed in full approbation by the US and US technical support.

Nevertheless, one little tweak by the US could scuttle Israeli security. While the Israeli army has built its image as a brutal, aggressive but yet

---

40   http://en.wikipedia.org/wiki/Israel_Military_Industries
       http://news.xinhuanet.com/english2010/world/2011-06/20/c_13938425.htm
41   http://news.xinhuanet.com/english/world/2012-07/28/c_131743749.htm

efficient fighting force, without US patronage and support that capacity would start to crack in a matter of a year or less.

> *"The US total of 44 per cent of the global arms market in 2010 rocketed to a staggering 79 per cent in 2011, mostly due to Middle East sales valued at some $56.3 billion that year."*

The Final Balance Sheet: US and Israel

The character of the US-Israeli relationship can be termed "dependent independence." The appearance is created of an independent Israel, but behind every policy announcement and statement can be read a US-supported stance. If Israel made a move militarily or in terms of foreign policy that was not pre-approved by the US, there would be an immediate reaction and correction of path by Washington. However, the US has taken measures at critical times, to reassure Israel about US intentions. An example is the US initiative to undertake joint minesweeping exercises with 25 countries in the Arabian Gulf in September 2012, taking care to confine the zone of operations just north of the strategic Straits of Hormuz[42]. This initiative is meant to increase military and political pressure on Iran and reassure Israel.

Israel's grandstanding on the international stage is precisely the cover they need to smokescreen their umbilical dependency on the US. So if Israel were to bomb Iranian nuclear facilities, this would have prior approval from Washington. Israel is in effect a lethal "forward deployed missile" of the US. The recent rhetorical attack by Prime Minister Benjamin Netanyahu on President Obama's reticence to set "red lines" vis-à-vis the Iranian nuclear situation has illustrated well, dissention is growing to Netanyahu's approach within the government and Israeli policy circles.

The US has also had a hard time recently in reining in Israel, first on Lebanon and now in Syria. It will become tougher for the US to control Israel's wish list of growth and expansion in the region. Growing pressure on Israeli leadership to make domestic territorial, political and economic

---

[42]   http://www.nytimes.com/2012/09/03/world/middleeast/us-is-weighing-new-curbs-on-iran-in-nod-to-israel.html?ref=world

concessions stems from an informal ghettoization of its population. Caucasian, Hasidic and African citizens of Israel are treated very differently in terms of opportunities and careers. Segregation along ethnic medians might eventually result in a increasingly disenfranchised population and escalating sociopolitical tensions.

No doubt Israel is a county that has achieved a lot in a short time, to an admirable degree. However, it is the US that leads the relationship without exception, and the growing tensions within Israel will provide the US with the required levers, checks and balances to continue to maintain control. Simultaneously, pressure within Israel will continue to factionalize the country along ethnic and religious-modernity fault lines.

President Obama has had a challenging time establishing a close relationship with Israel, even though he negotiated the Russians down from selling Iran an advanced anti-aircraft missiles system (hence allaying Israeli fears). After a few public gaffes, he put his direct contact with the tenacious Prime Minister Benjamin Netanyahu on ice, realizing that he could never win that war of image and words. The President judged that he could better spend his time dealing with myriad other foreign policy issues. However, the outcome of the November 2012 election and whether President Obama secures a second term in office will depend to a great extent on the American-Israeli Political Action Committee (AIPAC) and Israeli public lobbying. To that extent, the bid of President Obama to get reelected may have become a hostage of Israel.

Syria

At the beginning of this chapter, I described about the mosaic of communities in the Middle East and how a jigsaw of Muslim, Jewish, Christian and Orthodox sects interlace in a dynamic yet unstable mix. Nowhere is this more true than in Syria, where unique ethnic communities like the Druze and the Alawites add to fissures that divide communities rather than help them to congeal. Like Iraq and Lebanon, Syria has significant Shiite and Sunni populations intermingled with Orthodox and Christian; Lebanon and Syria also share a number of cross border ethnicities like the Alawites and the Druze.

Over the last decade, Syria has been in the news due to its strong Shiite connections with Iran and its support for the US-blacklisted Hezbollah in Southern Lebanon. Syria is now part of a band of Shiite-dominated states that includes Iran and Iraq, and aligns with Shiite communities in Jordan, Saudi Arabia, Bahrain, Qatar, UAE, Oman and Yemen.

> *"The regime change mantra is a good indication that the Obama Administration's objectives in Syria are limited to annulling Al-Assad as a support base for Iran and the larger Shiite regional politic, rather than medium term political reforms and eventual elections to bring democracy to Syria."*

Falling out of favor

In the era of Sadat, and in the US effort to secure its new best friend Israel, the US did not object to supporting the man who eventually ruled over Syria for decades and then passed the power scepter to his son, Bashar Al-Assad. Technically, Syria and Israel are still at war after the 1956 violent conflict, the occupation of Israel of Golan Heights, and the 2007 bombing by Israel of Syria's fledgling nuclear program. Practically apart from the 2007 bombing, the US negotiated a ceasefire in 1956 whereby both countries have lived by the status quo with Israel in occupation of Golan Heights for over 50 years[43].

In exchange, Al-Assad *pere* won immunity from overseas interference in his drive to consolidating power, eliminating all viable political opposition and building a powerful and networked secret service. The status quo was maintained through the decades and Assad's power was not challenged, even when extra-judicial kills and torture were hallmarks of his relentless rule. All through those decades, the US, UK and other Western powers never really championed the cause of human rights, the welfare of the people of Syria or of the representational aspects of democracy because the status quo with Israel was maintained and never threatened by Al-Assad. When the mantle of power was passed to Bashar, the US, UK and others

---

[43]   This section as many others in this book are drawn directly from the author's blog. http://opinionscan.me/2012/08/05/the-truth-about-syria-regional-spillover-and-theories-of-conflict-causes/

made sure that, as a prerequisite, Bashar signed on to the death pledge made by his father to secure Israel. In so doing he bought himself a decade of unchallenged rule.

Things started to go wrong for Bashar following the Hariri[44] assassination on 14 February 2005. Lebanon reacted violently and Syria, hitherto a security guarantor of sorts in Lebanon, was made to pull its military forces back across the border.

When the Arab Spring was sparked in Tunisia, it took little time to seed the sectarian unrest in Syria that led to the present civil war. The clear reading is that Bashar Al-Assad went too far with the Hariri assassination, and perhaps in other ways that are not in the public perview, upset the decades old balance with the US. The give-away lies in the Obama administration's constant and unequivocal calls for regime change, more puissant then their calls for a cessation of violence perpetrated on Syrian civilians by all sides.

The Arab Spring and Religious Extremist Movements

All Arab Spring movements, except in Yemen, have led to the election of parties or personalities linked to Islamic fundamentalist parties or principles. Tunisia narrowly missed electing a government that was fundamentalist dominated, but Egypt, Libya and Iraq all have seen religiously fundamentalist and aligned personalities rise to power. Except in Iraq, all the regimes are Sunni fundamentalist, drawing financing and constituency from extremist Wahhabi parties in Saudi Arabia and Salafi Sunni power brokers in Qatar, Kuwait and UAE.

Whether by design or by accident, the Arab Spring broke long-term dependency relationships between the US and the Middle East conglomerate of dictators that it supported and financed, opening the way for the US to shift its focus to the Asia-Pacific. One immediate result was the triggering of a religious fundamentalist political revival, Shiite and Sunni, all over the Middle East.

---

[44]   http://en.wikipedia.org/wiki/Rafic_Hariri

Syria will be no exception. Working through surrogates like Saudi Arabia and Qatar, the US is working to unseat the last dictator under the rubric of the old US-Middle East power pyramid and the Shiite axis of power: Bashar Al-Assad.

Regional Interference and Contagious Explosion of Syria

While Saudi Arabia, Qatar and Kuwait acted as surrogates for the US, they also had their own motivation of supporting the ascendency of Sunni leadership in Syria.

The current freedom struggle in Syria was fostered by support from those three neighboring states and Turkey. Financing for "study visits" to Saudi Arabia, for the Sunni community and for Sunni religious practice in Syria started to flow in abundance. Erstwhile marginalized Imams in mosques all over Syria are paid for travel and lavish hotel stays in Jeddah, Mecca and Medina, with shopping money thrown in. The declared purpose of these activities and financing for madrassas to be set up in Sunni mosques all over Syria is to bring the Syrians back into the mainstream of Sunni religious practice.

While in Saudi Arabia, these Imams and community leaders were given lectures and classes on how to organize civil disobedience. They met with representatives who talked about planning military campaigns, civil defense and inciting violence. They were offered training camps. There is no verification of the numbers involved or of the exact periodicity of the program, but there is also no means of dismissing the possibility that hundreds who accepted travel junkets also attended training camps or agreed to help start a violent rebellion in Syria[45].

On 24 July 2012, international news media[46] reported that Al Qaeda had approached freedom fighters in Syria to provide weapons and financial

---

[45] This information was received over a period of a year or so by the author from Syrian ex-colleagues that lived in the communities that were approached by Saudi Arabia and that participated.

[46] http://www.nytimes.com/2012/07/25/world/middleeast/al-qaeda-insinuating-its-way-into-syrias-conflict.html?pagewanted=all

support. This would significantly impact classification of the probable origins and trajectory of the rebel movement, which would then have its roots in regional interference rather than in a natural upswing of unrest. Violence and conflict has already started to seep from Syria into Saudi Arabia and is anticipated to spread to Kuwait, and re-ignite explosive Bahrain.

Meanwhile, in Turkey, the Alawite community still strongly supports Al-Assad and has criticized regional support for rebel movements within Syria. A spillover of the conflict, as has happened in Lebanon, is feared[47]. Turkey's concrete contribution to Syrian rebel movement is very controversial, as it compromises its status as a key member of NATO. The continued and growing involvement of Turkey and Saudi Arabia in Syria has the potential to explode, raising the specter of a larger Middle East war.

President Obama's Contribution

Given the longer-term contribution of the US to maintaining the Al-Assad family in power for over 50 years, it seems peculiar that the rare statements heard from Secretary of State Clinton and from President Obama are for regime change, and not an end to the violence and conflict. The regime change mantra is a good indication that the Obama Administration's objectives in Syria are limited to annulling Al-Assad as a support base for Iran and the larger Shiite regional politic, rather than medium term political reforms and eventual elections to bring democracy to Syria. No such suggestions have ever been uttered by the Obama team. Even though democratic reform elements appear in the Kofi Annan six-point peace plan, their importance was scrupulously downplayed when the former UN Secretary-General tried to get all the major actors to the table in Geneva[48], including Iran.

---

[47] http://www.nytimes.com/2012/08/05/world/middleeast/turkish-alawites-fear-spillover-of-violence-from-syria.html?pagewanted=all

[48] http://www.csmonitor.com/USA/Foreign-Policy/2012/0630/Not-much-progress-at-Geneva-meeting-on-Syria-violence

The inclusion of Iran in the negotiations have been categorically opposed by the State Department, even though they have publically acknowledged the key role that Iran plays vis-à-vis the deepening Syrian conflict. The Iran factor underscores the fact that the Obama administration's approach to Syria has been too shallow, narrow and lacking in a realistic historical and political foundation to be considered as a serious policy approach. The policy that appears to facilitate the sacrifice of thousands of Syrians is in itself a means to a larger US foreign policy objective to "getting" Iran.

Syria is already exploding, spilling venom in neighboring countries, fermenting the seeds for longer-term instability and igniting latent conflict factors like religious and political marginalization of minorities. In Syria, the once-complementary mosaic of religions and communities will give rise to protracted civil war until the majority Sunni dominate. Infrastructure and social fiber will be destroyed, taking generations to really heal and mend.

Globally, the failure of the international community to unite in action in the Security Council has not only spotlighted the consolidation of the P3 (US, UK, France), but also the diplomatic re-emergence of Russia and China. Due to the challenge of these two powers to the US over Syria, alignment with either is now perceived by the non-aligned countries as a viable alternative to alliance with the US.

Concluding Analysis

> *"Whether by design or by accident, the Arab Spring broke long-term dependency relationships between the US and the Middle East conglomerate of dictators that it supported and financed, opening the way for the US to shift its focus to the Asia-Pacific."*

Seven observations can close this chapter on US foreign policy in the Middle East, reflecting back on its introductory sections.

Firstly, US strategic interest in the Middle East is still centered on oil supplies, high levels of trade—particularly the arms trade—and maintenance of US military bases in Saudi Arabia and Bahrain.

Second, US strategy in the Middle East remains short-term. Even after the jolts and upheavals of the Arab Spring, the US maintains its main relationship line as military cooperation, and not the promotion of development or other aspects like human rights. The one exception is Israel. The US commitment to Israel remains long-term and trumps all other Middle Eastern considerations. The medium—and longer-term repercussion of this foreign policy short sightedness is the steady alienation of large swaths of Arab populations. The US is perceived not as a friend, but as a primary protagonist of violence, conflict, political repression and dictatorship.

Third, the duplicitous manipulation of the Sunni versus Shiite by US policy will implicitly create openings for China, Russia or other powers such as Brazil and India to form viable and lasting relationships in the Middle East. This is already in evidence in the case of China.

Fourth, unlike other Arab Spring conflicts, the Syrian civil war will have spillover effects in key US client states such as Saudi Arabia and Qatar, and also impact Turkey and Jordan. This impact is already visible in Lebanon.

Fifth, all these developments call into question the continued safety of Israel. If the US priority is Israeli stability, then the math on destabilization of four Israeli borders (Palestine, Egypt, Lebanon and Syria) should be a reason to thoroughly review US policy very soon.

Sixth, President Obama had a unique opportunity to transform the US-Iran relationship conclusively ending the zero-sum war of attrition that has been waging for the years since 1979. His policy of covert cyber warfare instead of personal engagement in crafting a deeper strategic approach towards Iran has resulted in a more tense and distrustful relationship then before.

Lastly, after the June 2009 speech in Cairo[49], in which President Obama promised a new era of friendship and development between the US and the

---

[49]   http://www.nytimes.com/2009/06/04/us/politics/04obama.text.
html?pagewanted=all

Middle East, he only engaged himself directly in the case of US withdrawal from Iraq. On Libya, President Obama took the step of listening to the then French President Nickolas Sarkozy, and together with the UK, the US pushed the Security Council to ask NATO to enforce a no-fly zone. Given that that region is passing through a process of democratic awakening, something that the US has promoted globally for over 100 years, the lack of personal engagement of President Obama in the Middle East is remarkable and highly questionable,

> *"So if Israel were to bomb Iranian nuclear facilities, this would have prior approval from Washington. Israel is in effect a lethal "forward deployed missile" of the US."*

Chapter 2

US Foreign Policy in the Near East and South Asia

Pakistan and Afghanistan are inextricably linked through common ethnicities, common languages and common cultures and religions. Events in one have an indelible effect on the other. Pakistan and India, one country until independence in 1947, share more than language, culture and bloodlines, they also share a deep-rooted aversion of each other based in the history of the Islamic conquest of India more then two centuries ago.

The US has been the key global power associated with the region and, except during the Soviet occupation of Afghanistan, it only has China as a regional rival. But US foreign policy has been inconsistent and not always positive in a region where hundreds of billions of dollars of military, development and social aid have been provided[50]. At times of divergence with Pakistan, aid has been cut off completely, but the relationship always struggles through and comes back to previously high levels. Concern with Afghanistan is a more recent phenomena. It didn't really appear on the US foreign policy screen until it was invaded by Soviet Union in December 1978; and then again with renewed intensity after 9/11.

The US relationship with India has strengthened only in the last decade as India emerged as a major economic and industrial power on global markets. The decades of diplomatic distance between the two countries

---

[50]   http://www.guardian.co.uk/global-development/poverty-matters/2011/jul/11/us-aid-to-pakistan
http://www.fas.org/sgp/crs/row/R41856.pdf

was predicated on India's close relationship with the Soviet Union, and India's reticence to open its economy and vast market potential to Western imported goods. All this changed in the 1990's as India's burgeoning and wealthy middle class became increasingly pro-Western. Today, India and the US have built a preferential trading and security relationship.

"Even after the jolts and upheavals of the Arab Spring, the US maintains its main relationship line as military cooperation, and not the promotion of development or other aspects like human rights."

PAKISTAN

The US-Pakistan relationship goes back to 1948. The conflict between India and Pakistan, a defining policy issue for Pakistan in terms of the strategically located Kashmir region, immediately caught post-war US's attention. Kashmir was a doorway to then-mysterious Central Asia and Western China.

At the time, India had definitive leanings towards socialism and the Soviet Union. Pakistan, an ideological state built on the dream of a few, remained neutral and was looking for friends in the "West". Wanting to balance growing Soviet influence in India, the US had a ready customer in Pakistan. The picture of assistance to Pakistan has not changed much to date including military assistance comprised of hardware and software (training and strategic command) and more importantly, intelligence and information gathering. In fact, the parent organization of the current Pakistan intelligence agency, ISI, was born of a US initiative to give Pakistan an intelligence structure through USAID and US Department of Defense assistance. The other aspect of US aid was developmental (health, education and agriculture), aimed at growing and stabilizing the country's industrial base.

The Non-Aligned Movement During the 1950s and 1960s, both Pakistan and India became very active in the Non-Aligned Movement[51]. NAM was supported by as an alliance by newly independent countries that consulted together to balance the bipolar politics of the US-Soviet

---

[51]   http://www.nam.gov.za/background/history.htm

cold war. There, Pakistan made significant contributions to the UN and to the then incipient South-South cooperation dialogue. This provided an opportunity for Pakistan to maintain its objectivity in foreign and global policy, often voting against US led initiatives in the UN and other milieu, and also supporting the rare statements or policies proposed by China.

Pakistan-China—a lasting relationship

During the same two decades, Pakistan attracted the attention of China, its northern neighbor. China was concerned with its tense border relationship with India and the need to balance the growing influence of the Soviet Union in that country. Pakistan-Chinese relations grew quickly, as Pakistan needed military assistance and training to maintain an edge over India. In the 1950s and 60s, only China was a likely provider based on Chinese motivation to secure a much-needed ally on its southern flank, neighboring its own volatile south-western region.

In the 1960's and 1970's, political rhetoric between the US and the Soviet Union took on global proportions and focused on communism versus capitalism, breading a newly virulent order of client states among newly independent countries in Africa, Latin America and Asia. China during the 1960s was still introverted in its politics, concentrating on countries that it considered within its sphere. Hence the Asian countries of Cambodia, Korea, Vietnam and others were all within China's priority interest, and were also locations where China clashed directly with the US sphere of influence[52].

Pakistan was not in the Korea-Vietnam boat. The China-Pakistan relationship provided China with a more neutral shoulder on which it could lean for about 10 years spanning the 1960-70s's; Pakistan was China's only neutral external ally. This worried the US that tried to build up its relations with Pakistan in an effort to draw Pakistan and China apart. While the US-Pakistan relationship grew, especially after the invasion of Afghanistan by the Soviet Union, the Pakistan-China relationship was maintained and strengthened by both those countries simultaneously.

---

[52]   http://www.foreignaffairs.com/articles/138009/andrew-j-nathan-and-andrew-scobell-how-china-sees-america

More recently, Pakistan is providing China with the warm water port they seek on the Arabian Gulf (Gwadar) and China is re-intensifying cooperation on military and development strategies with that country.

Evolving US-Pakistan Relations As part of the US effort to woo Pakistan, it decided early on to support the Pakistan military in a very tangible way, providing officer training for all ranks of military officers and command training for the high-ranking. The US also provided training for military officers in field intelligence, leading to a Pakistan intelligence capacity modeled, in the image of the CIA/FBI in the US, as an independent and sometimes supra-national entity barely subjected to any oversight or civil controls. The model of military assistance from the US, and the fact that Pakistan was prone to military coups and under military leadership from the early 1950s onwards, set up the dynamic for Pakistan to become a frontline US client state.

By the 1970s, a number of border disputes and wars between Pakistan and India had occurred, and India by now was a staunch Soviet ally.

Henry Kissinger took over the State Department and President Nixon the White House. By now, China is recognized as a balancing politico-military force to the Soviet Union and its forays into Cambodia, Vietnam and Korea. Pakistan, acting as go-between, negotiated a meeting between the US and China—the first manifestation of a US strategy of *détente* and directly contributing to diffusing tensions with China (this did not, however, eliminate the mutual distrust that continues to be a critical factor in the US-China relationship). The US-Pakistan relationship was cemented, giving it the *gravitas* necessary to endure repeated trials over decades up through the Obama drone wars. Till today, Pakistan is the informal negotiator and facilitator between China and the US during times when the US is not willing to publicize its dialogue on sensitive issues with China.

Two other issues made Pakistan indispensable to the US as a global and political ally: crises in Iran and Afghanistan.

The Iranian revolution followed hard on its heels by the US hostage crisis put Iran on the top of the "enemies of the state" list for the US—a location to which it returned recently, due to the controversy over its nuclear program. At no time during the last 30 years has Pakistan been more pertinent and important to the US policy than now. Pakistan would be the only reliable country to host US or NATO forces if longer-term military action or containment was to be envisioned in Iran. All other locations are too remote and would pose a huge logistical challenge for NATO. This assessment is supported by the logistics of NATO engagement in Afghanistan.

At the time of the invasion of Afghanistan by the Soviet Union, Pakistan intelligence officers were recruited and deployed within Afghanistan by the US. The ISI was formed as an independent agent with a regional mandate. Pakistan became the staging ground for a massive anti-Soviet and pro-liberation armed struggle in Afghanistan. Pakistanis and Afghanis who had escaped *en masse* to Pakistan as refugees were among the frontline fighters.

The military and financial assistance provided by the US at the time did not discriminate among recipients, and much of the funding went to religious communities within Pakistan who wanted to help Afghanis reclaim their country through a holy war: Jihad! Such was the beginning of the Jihadi movements in Pakistan. The Talibans were created as a religious fighting force and provided training, arms and support, principally by the US and Saudi Arabia, to liberate Afghanistan from godlessness, and to this day, they are doing exactly that. At the time, Pakistan was a most-favored nation and partner with the US.

When the Soviet occupation came to an end the US left abruptly, without helping or funding a post-liberation cleanup. This meant that new military and militant groups in Pakistan and Afghanistan with weapons, money and fighting power suddenly had nothing else to do but to insurrect, giving birth to Al-Qaeda. Many Pakistan-based organizations, and particularly the ISI, felt virtually abandoned by the US. They redirected their energies to new and old causes: India and Kashmir remained a battle cry; the new religious, right-wing organizations like Al-Qaeda and Lashker-E-Taiba became the new organizing units.

US policy in Pakistan The base of Pakistan's strategic value is its location as a gateway to China, Central Asia, Afghanistan, Iran, the Arabian Gulf and the Indian Ocean. Along the way, Pakistan (like India) became a nation that has proven and tested nuclear warhead capacity.

The proliferation of militaristic Islamic extremist organizations in Pakistan and their infiltration into all echelons of Pakistani society and government has raised fears that the Pakistan army, in charge of its nuclear arsenal, is equally infiltrated. If the US is concerned, it has so far not shown its hand in terms of foreign policy dialogue. If it is not concerned, then the rest of the world needs to worry about the US apathy on this very critical and potentially fatal subject. More so than in the case of Iran, Pakistan nuclear weapons are in danger of falling into "the wrong hands". The fact that Osama Bin Laden was for years hiding in Pakistan, presumably with the help of the US-fed ISI, leads to disturbing questions about accountability.

President Obama has only engaged Pakistan in the context of NATO deployments to Afghanistan and fighting terrorism, notably through drone wars and direct assaults, which resulted in hundreds of collateral civilian deaths according to Pakistan. In 2011, Obama made a critical choice not to consult or inform the Pakistanis before mounting *Operation Geronimo* (eradicating Osama Bin Laden), defining his tactical approach to Pakistan. But the cost to the US was high both in money and essential military supplies: Pakistan shut down NATO passage through its sovereign territory.

"At no time during the last 30 years has Pakistan been more pertinent and important to the US policy than now. Pakistan would be the only reliable country to host US or NATO forces if longer-term military action or containment was to be envisioned in Iran."

President Obama has not engaged Pakistan on other, more troubling problems that in the short and medium run are cause for real concern. These include the lack of democratization, extreme and entrenched systemic corruption, and it's nuclear arsenal. Pakistan is today a failed state on the verge of becoming a rogue nuclear state.

AFGHANISTAN

On 1 May 2012—the one-year anniversary of the mission that eliminated Osama bin Laden in Pakistan—President Obama flew to Afghanistan to sign the much-anticipated long-term Strategic Cooperation Agreement[53]. The President personally finalized details of the agreements and also discussed other issues of concern with President Hamid Karzai of Afghanistan in his palace in Kabul. This unprecedented agreement has significant implications for US-Afghan relations. More significantly, it sheds light on the Obama strategy for the Afghan neighborhood and the larger sub-region from 2014 to 2024. The fact that Obama personally travelled to Kabul signifies that the US is indicating a longer-term commitment to Afghanistan. Key allies, principally Pakistan and Iran, need to draw their own lessons.

NATO

Many NATO countries have indicated their desire to exit Afghanistan as soon as possible. Countries like France, the UK, Norway, Sweden and Australia have accelerated their troop withdrawals. President Obama's Strategic Agreement became a roadmap for the NATO summit in Chicago,[54] where commitments to the continued restructuring, capacity building and training of the Afghan national army and police were made. The Chicago summit[55] presented an opportunity for Afghanistan's European allies to underwrite the objectives of the US brokered strategic longer-term cooperation framework and set a timetable for withdrawal of their military contingents. This Obama move could prove to be a template, whereby NATO increasingly takes over military-civilian tasks while purely security issues remain the domain of US-client joint military forces.

---

[53] http://www.whitehouse.gov/sites/default/files/2012.06.01u.s.-afghanistanspasignedtext.pdf

[54] http://blogs.suntimes.com/sweet/2012/05/us-afgan_strategic_agreement_r.html

[55] http://www.nato.int/cps/en/natolive/official_texts_87593.htm?mode=pressrelease
http://www.consilium.europa.eu/uedocs/cms_Data/docs/pressdata/en/ec/130285.pdf

"Once the US downgrades its commitment to statecraft and rebuilding, who will foot the bills to keep Karzai in power?"

In the NATO ISAF declaration[56], the European commitment to the Longer-Term Strategy (2014-2024) has been significantly increased, despite Francois Hollande's election, Greece's possible withdrawal from the euro and Spain's 25 per cent unemployment rate and imminent banking collapse. In a tactical sense, the moderation of NATO's post-2014 assistance to Afghanistan implies a defeat for those within EU and NATO who wanted to use Afghanistan as a basis for expanded terms of reference for NATO in future.

Afghanistan represents the best chance for NATO to demonstrate its capacities in the realm of state building and peace building. The question is whether NATO would have a mandate and be operational in a new rebuilding and statecraft capacity, especially given the deepening Eurozone financial crisis. The challenge will also be for Afghanistan to control the rising tide of Talibanism infiltrating its own security forces if the NATO allies are going to continue to train and support their professionalization efforts as part of the new strategic plan. In September 2012, the US suspended joint training programs as the number of fatal attacks on locations hosting these session caused unacceptable NATO casualties[57].

The Chicago conference also implies a refocusing of regional alliances. Afghanistan is looking for money—Karzai has to finance his survival in Kabul and has to support a corrupt and inept bureaucracy to re-enter the country every time he travels. Once the US downgrades its commitment to statecraft and rebuilding, who will foot the bills to keep Karzai in power? Whatever the achievements so far in Afghanistan, NATO and the US have to look hard at a country that is resisting statehood, and that remains divided politically, regionally and ethnically; Afghanistan's many factions cannot coalesce to support a single national leader. The question is whether the Strategic Agreement will be enough to hold Afghanistan united and relatively stable in the face of a tradition of balkanization.

---

[56]   http://www.chicagonato.org/chicago-summit-declaration-news-40.php

[57]   http://www.nytimes.com/2012/09/03/world/asia/in-afghanistan-hitting-pause-on-local-police-training.html?pagewanted=all

The Region: Pakistan and Iran

Perhaps the most significant impact of the new strategic plan will fall on Pakistan. The Strategic Agreement effectively relegated the need to consult with or to involve Pakistan in any future Afghan strategy. It can be read as a clear slap in the face to Pakistan, indicating that the US will continue to pursue the very tactics that the Pakistanis have found objectionable: drone strikes and cross-border bombing. This will change the US relationship with Pakistan conclusively and it will also have implications, perhaps not immediate, on the total US assistance package of development and military aid. The fall out will be enormous and perhaps positive, in that it may convince Pakistan to institute much-needed governance reforms.

The passive attitude adopted by Pakistan President Zardari during the Chicago conference illustrates Pakistan's finesse in biding its time. The US president was allowed to go through announcements and photo opportunities before re-initiating, at America's request, bilateral negotiations. Zardari countenanced Pakistan's marginalization from the main future reference set for Afghanistan only to later open the way for bilateral agreements for NATO's safe passage to Afghanistan via Pakistan. In Chicago, Pakistan effectively sat back and allowed itself to be played back in by not making expected concessions to the Americans. At the core of Pakistan's strategy is the certain knowledge that geo-strategic location will ensure it will be in demand as long as the US and NATO have a role in Afghanistan. To implement the longer-term agreement itself, Pakistan will remain pivotal.

Another reason for Pakistan's centrality to any Near East strategy, as has already been indicated, is Iran. Proximity to Iran is a key benefit of this Afghan Strategic Agreement; it provides the US and NATO with another means of applying indirect pressure. While nuclear negotiations are stalled, this Agreement gives the US a key foothold in the region and boots-on-the-ground for another 10 years.

US Foreign Policy in Afghanistan

The Strategic Longer-term Afghanistan Agreement is a coup for President Obama and shows that his personal involvement and engagement in planning foreign policy pays off. This mechanism provides the US with a tactical and strategic edge on Afghanistan, Pakistan and Iran, and allows the US and NATO key capacities in monitoring these quasi-rogue states.

The overall US foreign policy and engagement in Afghanistan has undergone a sea change under the Obama presidency, one that withdraws a majority of American and NATO forces from a fruitless ground war in an inhospitable country, yet allowing NATO a means of supporting peace-building efforts. With this one Agreement, President Obama reduced exposure of the US armed forces but gave the Afghanis a sense of longer-term security and support.

The US also tried to use the Agreement to admonish Pakistan but in the short-run, that did not work. Eventually US had to meet all the conditions laid down by Pakistan for a resumption of NATO transport through the Khyber Pass. At the same time, the mission to eliminate Osama Bin Laden and the marginalization of Pakistan at Chicago redoubled the conviction in Pakistani policy circles that China and not the US is their only really long-term friend. Afghanistan remains a country seeking a way to coalesce as a nation, while Pakistan has become a failed but nuclear—capable state more cautious with the US and much warmer to China.

INDIA

"More so than in the case of Iran, Pakistan nuclear weapons are in danger of falling into "the wrong hands"."

The economy of the most populous democracy in the world is showing some signs of slowing, posting a first quarter growth rate of 1.3 per cent; from 2000-2012 the average annual growth rate of India was 7.4 per cent.[58], External economic shocks will impact India in the future but to a much lesser extent than other tiger economies because of its huge internal market, and to a growing number of Asians, Africans and Latin Americans whose tastes are more attuned to Bollywood then to Hollywood. India's quest for oil and mineral resources has made it change its approach to a number of African countries; today, India is giving technical development

---

[58]   http://www.tradingeconomics.com/india/gdp-growth

advice through its embassies in countries facing diverse economic and social challenges, ranging in location from Central and West Africa to Bolivia.

India's political approach remains very much rooted in the tradition of the Non-Aligned Movement. It is a centrist, non-violent approach that reaches out to traditional opponents (Pakistan and China) as well as historic allies (Russia and Eastern Europe) with the same measure of constructivism backed by a firm sense of self-interest.

Recently, India has embarked on a strenuous upgrading of its navy and submarine fleets[59] with China in mind[60]. India and the US have reached an in-principle agreement to share patrolling the Bay of Bengal, the South China Sea and the Indian Ocean. While India will have a defined military strategy to inform its patrolling activities, this measure marks an innovation in the military relationship and collaboration between India and the US. The recently announced joint India-China naval exercises[61] have come as a surprise to the US, and deeply underscore the independence of India's foreign and strategic policy. While India agreed to naval cooperation with the US, it also sees a different and pragmatic path to easing tension with China in the South China Sea and in the Indian and Pacific oceans

Another realm of cooperation lies in Afghanistan and Pakistan. India and the US have more to share in the management of these two failed states than any other countries. The deepening relations between China and Pakistan have alarmed New Delhi. India sees the Gwadar port development initiative in Pakistan by China as placing the Chinese military and navy too close to Indian borders for comfort. Perhaps the agreement to conduct joint maneuvers with China is intended to deescalate the Gwadar threat.

---

[59] http://www.upi.com/Top_News/Special/2012/04/02/India-upgrades-submarine-fleet/UPI-42081333372730/
http://www.worldpoliticsreview.com/trend-lines/11373/global-insider-despite-outpacing-competitors-indias-navy-seeks-to-upgrade

[60] http://www.navytimes.com/news/2012/02/ap-india-upgrades-its-military-with-china-in-mind-020812/

[61] http://www.nytimes.com/2012/09/05/world/asia/india-and-china-agree-to-resume-joint-military-exercises.html?_r=1

Where the US and India part ways is with regard to Iran. Faced with US-imposed financial sanctions on Iran but wanting to maintain critical oil supplies from that source, India preferred to work out an Indian Rupee payment scheme with Iran rather then comply fully with the US' scheme for complete financial isolation. This well illustrates the balance that India will always strike in its relations with the US, and its own need for internal economic and social growth.

"Where the US and India part ways is with regard to Iran."

Chapter 3

US Foreign Policy in Africa

". . . the failure of the international community to unite in action in the Security Council has not only spotlighted the consolidation of the P3 (US, UK, France), but also the diplomatic re-emergence of Russia and China."

When President Bill Clinton signed the *Africa Growth and Opportunity Act*[62] on 18 May 2000, his initiative was greeted with a significant amount of skepticism. Yet big business and resource exploration corporations and the oil industry got behind the vast opportunity that the AGOA and Africa opened up. In the Bush years, AGOA came to define the cornerstone of US foreign policy towards Africa.

Following President Clinton, President Bush complemented AGOA by the redefining US strategic and military policy under AFRICOM[63]. This initiative prioritized military support, assistance and US military cooperation for such priority initiatives such as the eradication of Lord's Resistance Army (LRA)[64] and the rooting out of Al-Shabab[65] movement from Somalia and from East Africa. President Obama therefore inherited, the strongest US commitment to Africa in terms of foreign, commercial and military commitment since the end of the Cold War.

---

62   http://www.agoa.gov
63   http://www.africom.mil
64   http://www.globalsecurity.org/military/world/para/lra.htm
65   http://en.wikipedia.org/wiki/Ash-Shabaab (Somalia)

Under President Obama, the commitment to Africa has not flagged and has certainly expanded as high 6-8 per cent growth rates on the continent continued to entice US corporations to what amounts to new markets with full appetites for US goods. Yet a host of challenges facing business and foreign direct investment in Africa had allowed the AGOA only to benefit those countries that have worked hard to put in place minimum business-friendly commercial and financial reforms like Ghana, and those that are resource-rich such as Gabon.

Missing in this discourse is any conditionality on human rights, democratization and improving rule of law and the quality of the people-to-government social contract that defines the quality of governance, replicating the mistakes and gaps of US policy over the last three decades in the Middle East. These lessons can be hard to apply when business is defined in purely corporate terms. However in Africa, the US already has experience from its Cold War days, when US competition with the Soviet Union played itself out through a series of entrenched conflicts as the Angolan Civil War, occupation of South West Africa or Namibia, and propagation of such dictators such as Mobutu Sese Seko in Zaire (today's DRC).

CHALLENGES TO DOING BUSINESS IN AFRICA

International businesses continue to face significant challenges on the ground in Africa. Part of the challenge is the lack of experience in the US of whom to do business within Africa. The challenges can be summarized as:

- systemic corruption and nepotism, including entrenched structural weaknesses such as elite politico-economic and ownership structures;
- antiquated and complicated financial and commercial laws; limited and hard to build up physical, social and business infrastructural networks, including roads and free markets;
- diverse linguistic/cultural orientations and business culture.

Africa's Potential

The allure of the seemingly limitless natural, mineral and energy resources, most of which remain marginally explored or still virgin, trump the many challenges. Africa has three strong factors that make it a target for US business:

- abundant resources: natural, mineral and energy;
- a youth bulge: 60% of the population of Sub-Saharan Africa is below 30 years old.

The starting point of today's commercial ventures is in its infancy: a majority of African countries do not possess adequate commercial and business experience or manpower to support the growth of commerce and markets within their economic grasp, opening lucrative employment markets for US graduates looking for jobs. This also presents business opportunity to companies specializing on building up business architecture and infrastructure

Despite some Cold War baggage, the US is not tainted with the European heritage of colonialism that can discourage African engagement with former colonial masters.

AFRICOM and the Political Agenda in Africa

The economic and business agenda is not detached from the political and military relationships that the US promotes in Africa.

The political engagement of the US in Africa is defined by its guilt-ridden relations with Rwanda and East Africa (Somalia Black Hawk Down). Military cooperation through AFRICOM has mirrored this reality. For the first time since Somalia, US military put boots-on-the-ground in Uganda to train the Ugandan National Army to fight and eliminate the threat posed by the LRA. In East Africa, the US Army and intelligence deployed officers to support the fight to control Somali pirates working in the Indian Ocean. They also deployed some training and technical staff to Ethiopia and Kenya to support the engagement of regional forces fighting inside Somalia to rout Al-Shabab forces around Mogadishu. In a number of other countries, the US government and military are investing technical expertise and know-how as "consultants" to help shape and implement, security sector reform efforts so critical to professionalizing antiquated African armies, and decreasing the potential for military-sponsored coups.

Yet contrary to the lessons that should have been learned from almost four decades of mistakes in the Middle East, the US is including very little conditionality in its financial, commercial and military relationships on critical issues such as good and transparent governance, strengthening human rights and the rule of law, and promoting political pluralism and political transparency in Africa. Thus far the pattern of US dialogue has emulated their decades old practice in countries like Egypt, Yemen and Saudi Arabia of supporting despotic dictatorships to remain in power to serve US foreign policy interests.

Two of the countries where this is most evident is in the Democratic Republic of Congo and Gabon, both extremely resource rich partners for the US with abysmal governance and human rights records. Conditionalities on human rights, a hallmark of the unpopular Jimmy Carter presidency, still remain necessary in Africa, a continent that continue to register the highest number of human rights violations on the individual and community level. These have not been voiced in US policy approaches towards a continent that has a good chance and a history of producing malevolent dictators and protracted wars.

THE GREAT LAKES: DRC, RWANDA AND UGANDA

DEMOCRATIC REPUBLIC OF CONGO

The situation in the Eastern DRC is fast approaching the insecurity of 2003/2004 and of 2007/2008, when both Kivus provinces were caught in a vicious cycle of violence perpetrated by a profusion of armed groups, both of Congolese and Rwandan origin. Today, Congo is once again facing increasing insecurity, fast proliferating armed and self-defense groups, and violent skirmishes leading to significant and multiple population displacements. Threats have been noted not only in the east but also in the west of Congo.

The UN has been on the ground for nearly 12 years and has done a lot to support the country in its bid to stabilize, foster state institutions and a working parliament, and start the arduous process of peace building. However, over the last two years, the situation has started to unravel with the Goma peace accords of 2008 (the cornerstone of UN's security and stabilization strategy in the East) in tatters. ICG's Open Letter to the Security Council[66] stating that MONUSCO needs urgently to review its strategy is straight on target.

Given the growing challenges to peace and security, MONUSCO would be advised to overhaul its approach and its objectives in the next phase of its operations in the DRC, in order to support the Congolese people to stabilize the situation, decrease violence and human rights violations, encourage freedom of movement and most importantly, start to rebuild the confidence and the relationship of the people of Congo with its Government, in an irreversible manner. MONUSCO's current stabilization policy was developed under the premise that conflict was in abeyance. Now, with sexual and gender-based violence (SGBV) and armed attacks against unarmed civilian populations increasing at an alarming rate, any notion that the conflict in DRC is abating is an illusion.

The Kivus

The Kivus are the victims of violence, greed and possession from all the neighbors. They have attracted war, rape and killing throughout recorded history, due to the high amount of natural and mineral resources that are hidden in DRC's fertile land. After the first and second Congolese war spanning over almost two decades in the 1990's-2000's, the people of the Kivus have been traumatized, raped and battered, but still somehow retain the will to recommence and turn their backs on the past.

In 2012, an acceleration in the calls to action the ICC arrest warrant[67] against the National Congress for the defense of the People (CNDP) leader Bosco Ntaganda, led to Kinshasa's hesitation to continue to grant

---

[66] http://www.crisisgroup.org/en/publication-type/media-releases/2012/ africa/dr-congo-open-letter-to-unsc.aspx

[67] http://www.haguejusticeportal.net/index.php?id=9467

him impunity and protect him. Weeks later, Movement 23 (M23), a sub-group of CNDP, emerged and threw North and South Kivu into conflict, causing millions to displace inside and outside the DRC.

M23's demands revolve around the inability of the Kinshasa government to honor and implement their commitments under Goma Peace agreements, and it is based on the coincidence of a huge increase of financial and military support from Kagame's Rwanda[68], and a need to gain protection from arrest for Bosco. M23 can walk into Goma anytime, as they occupy the surrounding areas. Whether they will occupy Goma remains to be seen as a very high number of Rwandan merchants and mineral traders access valuable resources in the markets of Goma as about 60 per cent of all Goma-based trade financially benefits Rwanda.

Secondly, diplomats from the US and UK were evacuated from Goma in August 2012, and UN personnel deployed in MONUSCO are on stand-by to be taken out. A take over of Goma now would just provide more ammunition to Kinshasa and the international community against the M23 and the role of their parent organization CNDP in destabilizing DRC, while not materially enhancing M23/Rwanda's position or assets in any way.

In August 2012, the M23[69] consolidated their control over the border municipalities of Rutshuru and Massisi, and also tightened their occupation of critical areas around Goma in what amounts to a military encirclement and an occupation. Supported by neighboring Rwanda with recruits, arms and ammunitions, the M23 have reversed the tentative and fragile peace in Eastern DRC, by forcing the Government to own up to its own failure to comply with and implement in a timely way, commitments made under the Goma Peace Agreements of 2008. The success of M23 has also highlighted the failure of the Congolese National Army (the FARDC) to defend its national territory against aggression.

---

[68] http://www.provincenordkivu.org/doc9/Rapport_des_experts_des_NU_-_annexe_-_Addendum_(26_June_2012)FINAL[1].pdf

[69] http://www.chicagotribune.com/news/sns-rt-us-congo-massacresbre87s0uy-20120829,0,6457089.story

Unfortunately, M23's earlier demands of dialogue and negotiations directly with the Government that had been accepted by President Kabila, are in peril of being sabotaged by the recent increase in violence around Goma that is attributed to M23. President Kabila is working with an incompetent army and some of the highest levels of state corruption in Africa. He has also succeeded in upsetting all his erstwhile regional allies including Angola and Zimbabwe, who in the past came to his assistance to restore state control militarily in the East.

Over last two years, tensions have been rising within Burundi as the ruling party and President arrested and restricted opposition parties in the lead up to contested elections. The increasing political acrimony has meant that armed groups such as the National Force of Liberation (FNL) that operated partially from DRC's South Kivu[70] and maintained strong alliances with Congolese Mai Mai groups and the Democratic Forces for the Liberation of Rwanda (FDLR), have been resurgent in gaining support from the rural Burundians and remilitarizing their members in preparation for larger remonstrations.

But increasing militarization is only part of the reason why Burundi is going to be the second Great Lakes country to return to conflict. The main reason is that the Tutsi minority retaining controlling positions in the army, police and secret service have gotten direct political and material support from Kagame's Rwanda, not surprising if Kagame's Tutsi nationalism is to be realized.

Allegedly, the tightening of liaison between Rwanda and Burundi Tutsi networks has pushed their Hutu counterpart in government and the armed forces to admit the failure of the peace process, and initiate countermeasure strategies. For DRC, this indicates that Kagame might have negotiated an access route through Burundi to South Kivu through Burundian Tutsi elements[71].

---

[70] http://www.scribd.com/doc/97990059/UN-DRC-Group-of-Experts-Interim-Report-21-Jun-2012

[71] The author received this information from Burundian Military officers in active service.

Kagame's plan is apparently to infiltrate South Kivu taking over Bukavu and Uvira (South Kivu's two main cities) whether directly or through surrogates, in an extension of their occupation of North Kivu. FNL now resurgent in their logistic bases in Fizi (South Kivu) and other border areas of South Kivu. FNL is allegedly working with FDLR and the Mai Mai to try to mount a defense where Kabila's army seems impotent to defend their people.

This sets the stage for a larger destabilization of Eastern Congo. After South Kivu, Northern Katanga and southern Ituri will also be drawn into quasi-occupation, as Rwanda seeks to extend access to natural resources (gold in Ituri) and vital transport through Lake Tanganyika. It is only a matter of time before the situation in the East flares from war and displacement to a fight to maintain the territorial integrity of the DRC.

Kinshasa and the Kabila Government

The knock-on effects are already clear on the sustainability of the Kabila Government: the President fears for his life while his isolation from the Kinshasa-based political environment (parliament and his own party members), the East and the West is virtually complete. A coup d'etat by his army officials, his party or others is now more a reality than a mere possibility. The fact that he is so isolated and on such "thin ice" nationally and regionally harks back to the end of Mobutu Sese Seko's days in the old Zaire.

Kabila has approached Angola and Zimbabwe for military help and support but it will cost him dearly.

Angola was rebuffed heavily by Kabila after the 2006 election and after they intervened militarily last in March 2007 during Jean Pierre Bemba's challenge to Kabila's presidency. Since then, relations have been crumbling. Now Angola is asking for *de facto* open borders in Bas Congo (one way for traffic from Angola) and very compromising concessions to the lucrative oil waters off Matadi's coast in exchange for limited military support.

Zimbabwe, stuck in its own process, has set a high monetary price for their military intervention, something cash-poor Kabila cannot meet. He doesn't have money to pay the salaries of his Republican Guards on whom he depends heavily to protect him and keep him in power—they have been raiding restaurants and local populations in their zones of deployment to get food.

Kabila appears to be stuck in a downward spiral, which will inevitably swallow all of DRC unless he acts now to loosen constraints on the parliamentary and democratic processes, and gets the UN to step up their activities in support of peace consolidation. The last six years since the 2006 elections has been valuable time lost to Congo, primarily due to Kabila's lack of leadership and inability to control corruption and nepotism that succeeded in stifling all development and progress in the country. New initiatives now to prove he can be a fit President might be "too little too late" for Kabila.

The West

The opposition party UDPS technically won the elections according to many observation reports from EU, UN itself and independent observers. After the final counting however, Kabila was able to retain power in what amounted to, corrupt 2011 elections. The marginalization of UDPS further enraged and isolated the Western provinces from Kinshasa, the later being perceived as being dominated by the Katangese.

But as far back as 2009, the cracks between Kinshasa and the West emerged as evidenced by the Enyele[72] revolution. That movement was dismissed and then suppressed by Kabila unfortunately using UN logistics as a means of support for FARDC units that indiscriminately killed and violated Equateur populations.

The province of Bas Congo is not far behind in terms of significant state sponsored violence against local political movements, such as the Bundu Dia Kongo Military (BDM). This has resulted in the increasing militarization of the West. While not immediate, the concerns of the Western provinces are rising and will find a voice at a high price to the

---

[72]   http://www.african-bulletin.com/watch/449-drc-arrest-of-the-enyele-rebel-leader.html

DRC, if remedial measures and some fair representation of Western political parties is not immediately under taken.

The recent decision to work with South Africa to repair the Inga Dam hydroelectric facility[73] was a wise decision by President Kabila. He bought time to resolve the security-political issues by showing that the South Africans are invested in Congo, and the deal provides hope in Western Congo for jobs, electricity and development.

The Conclusion

The DRC is Africa's most active political and conflict environment. Its current trajectory is moving the country towards longer-term conflict and destabilization; the very high investments of the international community over the last 12 years in (MONUC/MONUSCO) seems to be marking significant reversals recently, particularly in 2012.

At the same time, the regional appetite for a share if not outright ownership of Congolese land and resources is growing, and is at the heart of interference not only from Rwanda but also Uganda and others. This vast ungoverned land is a natural heaven on earth but it is fraught with conflict and the lack of governance capacity. Corruption is eating away at any intentions to create a nation in the heart of Africa. International mining businesses are also in the game, financing candidates and processes that will support their exploration and extraction operations in DRC[74].

Despite all this, Syria and Iran have eclipsed international attention to a very expensive problem, when (and not if) it comes to pass: the dissolution of the DRC. Right now the Security Council should be considering measures to support consolidating the territorial integrity of the DRC and urging the UN Mission to report more truthfully and accurately in real-time about events not only in the east and Kinshasa but also in the west.

---

[73] http://www.waterpowermagazine.com/story.asp?storyCode=2061134

[74] http://www.miningweekly.com/article/drc-gold-miner-declares-commercial-production-2012-08-29

If the world now turns a blind eye to DRC, the cost will be heavy. Burundi and eventually Rwanda will fall under the compelling infectiousness of Congo's destabilization, while increasing political instability and friction in countries like Uganda and South Sudan raise the specter of a larger war in the heart of Africa.

The next steps is for the US and President Obama to take Rwanda to task for its intervention in the DRC, but simultaneous the UN needs to increase its support and reporting to the Security Council on the broader regional dimensions of destabilization in the Great Lakes and Central Africa.

RWANDA

"Yet contrary to the lessons that should have been learned from almost four decades of mistakes in the Middle East, the US is including very little conditionality in its financial, commercial and military relationships on critical issues such as good and transparent governance, strengthening human rights and the rule of law, and promoting political pluralism and political transparency in Africa."

Rwanda has been a model nation when it comes to demonstrated results with post-conflict recovery, re-building infrastructure, schooling and health services. One of the only countries in Africa aggressively pushing gender mainstreaming, Rwanda has a higher then 50 per cent female participation in governance and public life.

Until recently, President Paul Kagame was considered one of Africa's enlightened leaders. During the last elections, his reputation was tarnished due to the arbitrary arrests, willful persecution and unexplained assassination of a majority of political opposition parties and personalities, regardless of the legality of their registration as an election candidate.

Worse, the dogged legacy of Rwanda's role in the first and second Congolese wars in which millions of Congolese were killed, has returned as today, Rwanda is accused of supporting a new rebel movement led by a ICC indicted war criminal in the Eastern Congolese province of North Kivu.

Rwanda's Intervention in the DRC

Since the 1994 Genocide, and the pushing back of the *Genocidaires*[75] into Eastern Congo by the liberating forces of General Paul Kagame, Rwanda has been a "frequent visitor" to Eastern Congo. Uninvited and unwanted by the local Congolese populations, following the Genocide, Rwanda invaded North Kivu to pursue their own persecutions of Hutu genocidaires[76].

Rwanda's intervention triggered over a decade of war, violence and mayhem that resulted in the death of hundreds of thousands of Congolese civilians. This black period of Congolese history is called the first Congolese war[77]. Some years later in 1998, the Zairian state began to disintegrate under the weight of Mobutu's massive corruption and huge manipulations of people, power and military. Attracted by the enormous natural and mineral wealth of Congo, almost all neighboring countries became embroiled in the conflict, which finally claimed some 5.4 million Congolese lives. This became known as the Second Congolese war. Rwanda bore a huge part of the blame[78] but Uganda and others were also involved and responsible.

In more recent times, Rwanda continues to sponsor and finance armed groups in Eastern Congo. CNDP and General Laurent Nkunda was the chief officer responsible for pillaging, raping and killing thousands of Congolese; he was operating directly under orders from Kigali and general Kagame, who by this time was President Paul Kagame of Rwanda[79].

---

[75] Hutu perpetrators of the 1994 Rwandan genocide

[76] Gerard Prunier *Africa's World War: Congo, The Rwandan Genocide and the Making of a Continental Catastrophy* Oxford university Press 2009, New York.

[77] http://en.wikipedia.org/wiki/First_Congo_War

[78] http://en.wikipedia.org/wiki/Second_Congo_War

[79] http://en.wikipedia.org/wiki/National_Congress_for_the_Defence_of_the_People

Currently, the M23 led by Bosco Ntaganda and also supported by Paul Kagame of Rwanda[80], is again causing hundreds of thousands of people to displace, indiscriminately killing and plunder, North Kivu's border territories with Rwanda.

The Security Council has to take a stand against repeated Rwandan interference and support for armed groups inside the DRC, in a way to pre-empt the further exacerbation of the causes of conflict to result in a third Congolese war, and the physical disintegration of the country.

UGANDA

In October 2011, President Obama announced the deployment of 100 US marines to support the Ugandan National army to plan, deploy and eliminate the Lord's Resistance Army leader Joseph Kony[81]. By February 2012, US military support to the dismantling of LRA and the "kill or capture" of Joseph Kony had expanded to operations covering four Central African countries, covering terrain the size of California[82].

After decades of violence, abductions, rapes, killing and torture in Uganda, South Sudan and Democratic Republic of Congo, LRA had finally been noticed by many socially conscious American tourists to Uganda; they decided to raise awareness of the continuing brutality of the LRA through videos and testimonials in documentaries and U-Tube video films. This created a huge outcry in the US and the Whitehouse decided to support frontline states to manage intelligence and ground operations to eradicate the menace posed by LRA. While results on the ground have been good, in the first US military deployment to Africa after the aborted Somali "Black Hawk Down", the US has marked a success in terms of on-the-ground collaboration across four African national armies and in achieving the objective of ridding Central Africa and Uganda of the LRA.

---

[80] http://www.scribd.com/doc/97990059/UN-DRC-Group-of-Experts-Interim-Report-21-Jun-2012

[81] http://www.bbc.co.uk/news/world-africa-15317684

[82] http://www.armytimes.com/news/2012/02/ap-us-troops-fighting-lra-in-4-african-countries-022212/

Yet US support to Musevini's Uganda was concretely linked to Uganda's pledge and military deployment to fight the Al-Shabbab rebels in Somalia. Kenya and Uganda together with Ethiopia make up the bulk of the African forces deployed to stabilize that war-torn country. Both engagements have meant that Uganda is a recipient of US military assistance, including military hardware and software. The extent of Ugandan involvement in the fight to eradicate the Al-Shabab rebels was deepened after Al-Shabbab claimed responsibility[83] for at least two bombings killing innocent Ugandan civilians in Kampala. More recently, Uganda has had a major set back when three Ugandan helicopters crashed in Kenya on their way to deploy to Somalia[84].

The US engagement in Central Africa in eradicating the LRA and the low-level US military and intelligence support to operations against the Al-Shabbab and Somali privates in Somalia are indicative of a shift in US policy in Africa to a slow and cautious return to that arena of US military presence.

This re-opening to Africa has the hallmarks of President Obama's own interest even though US cooperation in Somalia began under President Bush. The re-emergent US interest in supporting Africa to fight entrenched conflict is a very positive sign and needs to be recognized and applauded.

SOUTH AFRICA

The Obama Administration has made a great effort to woo South Africa. Secretary of State Hillary Clinton has conducted two official visits and in 2011, First Lady Michelle Obama spent a lengthy time touring that country.

However, during the last four years, South Africa has shown a spirit of independence and non-alignment with the US in particular, on a number of issues, including Libya and now Iran. A heavy weight in Africa politics,

---

[83] http://www.washingtonpost.com/wp-dyn/content/article/2010/07/12/AR2010071200476.html

[84] http://www.usatoday.com/news/world/story/2012-08-23/uganda-somalia-unrest/57238980/1

in April 2011, South Africa joined the BRIC, in an acknowledgement of the global significance of the South African economy and their potential political role in any emerging alliance.

South Africa has often resisted US efforts at the African level and at the global level to bully it into joining crusades against one or another country, instead choosing to advocate a path of negotiation and mediation. This might also draw from the traditional support that post-apartheid South Africa has shown for Palestine; the PLO was one of the major political and military supports to the ANC's fight against apartheid when few stood with that organization to achieve its objectives of eradicating apartheid[85]. While South Africa maintains good relations with Israel, they always support the Palestinian call for a two state solution and an end to the enforced isolation of the West Bank.

South Africa has itself appointed a number of high-level mediators to help the AU and the UN with countries in conflict or those facing political transitions, such as Burundi and Somalia. Their well-trained and high caliber civil services also support African countries to strengthen their governance structures and security services through bilateral programs of cooperation.

South Africa is very involved in security sector reform on the continent and is helping difficult countries like the DRC to restructure their command-and-control capacities. In August 2012, South Africa and DRC announced the setting up of a exploratory commission to study the ways and means of upgrading and rehabilitating the Inga Dam, a hydroelectric power facility that potentially has the scope to provide very reasonably priced energy to most of Southern Africa. Such a project would finesse South Africa's growing challenge to provide well paying jobs for its still semi-trained workforce and to take the lead in stabilizing a key Central African country, the DRC.

Finally, South Africa absented from voting on the Syria resolutions in the Security Council, showing its unwillingness to align behind the US, UK

---

[85]   http://www.bdssouthafrica.com/2012/02/sa-pledges-support-for-palestinians-mel.html

and France on their proposed way forward in that country. Rather, South Africa supported Egypt's President Mursi's initiative to lead a regional mediation excluding the US, UK and France on Syria. Growing caution would well describe South Africa's attitude and approach to US foreign policy, while the US seeks to enhance its cooperation with that country economically and politically.

US Foreign Policy Towards the Great Lakes

"The US engagement in Central Africa in eradicating the LRA and the low-level US military and intelligence support to operations against the Al-Shabbab and Somali privates in Somalia are indicative of a shift in US policy in Africa to a slow and cautious return to that arena of US military presence."

The US has been nursing its guilt for not acting to save lives during the genocide in Rwanda in 1994. Since 1995, it has flooded Rwanda with financial and development assistance critical for that country to rebuild its physical and social infrastructure. So dedicated has been US support for Rwanda and its President Kagame, that to a great extent, the US has led a group of important countries, notably the UK, to be blindsided to the impact of Rwandan interference in the DRC.

Rwanda's direct military and financial support and intervention in the DRC caused 5.4 million Congolese to be killed between 1994 and 2000. Then again in 2003/4, Rwandan backed CNDP rebels led by Laurent Nkunda invaded North and South Kivu killing, torturing, raping and pillaging millions of villages, causing massive death and displacement of local Congolese populations.

The M23 directly backed by Rwanda and investigated by the UN Security Council Group of Experts is again destabilizing the whole of Eastern Congo and spinning violence out of control. The US should ensure that Rwanda is fully accountable for its destructive role in the DRC and corrective measures have to be deployed immediately, through the UN, to secure DRC's territorial integrity as a priority.

The beneficial relationships and great industry that the AGOA has engendered all over Africa, thanks to the US is energizing small business, innovation and reform aimed at making business and transparency a priority.

Yet the success of the US in this area and in re-opening to Africa in initiatives such as the eradication of LRA and the Al-Shabbab, will be overshadowed by the lack of US engagement to secure the DRC and to take Rwanda to task for its negative and destructive conduct in that country. The longer that the US delays action to rectify Rwanda's misplaced interventions, the more the global community will be forced to acknowledge that Rwanda is now a pariah state, feeding off the misery and violence perpetrated on the people of Congo.

Rwanda is a candidate country for a non-permanent seat on the Security Council for the coming two-year period, but while it directly supports violence and war in neighboring DRC, Rwanda should never be allowed to take up such a position. President Obama is invited to take this case up personally and ensure that justice and stability return to the DRC.

Key African countries like South Africa and Nigeria have shown a growing independence of US as well as British and French foreign policy initiatives over the last decade in the UN Security Council. The trend is towards increasing divergence from the US on policy and strategic issues and convergence with the BRIC plus group (Brazil, Russia, China, India, Indonesia, Malaysia, Venezuela, Chile, Argentina and others).

Conclusions

"The Security Council has to take a stand against repeated Rwandan interference and support for armed groups inside the DRC, in a way to pre-empt the further exacerbation of the causes of conflict to result in a third Congolese war, and the physical disintegration of the country."

While the US should definitely maintain its engagement with Africa, the US can also integrate key lessons learnt from the Middle East and South Asia. Africa is still at a simpler stage of evolution than these other regions both politically and commercially. But it has a complicated heritage of history and inter-community conflict that underscores the need for a more holistic and conscientious US strategy and policy.

There is a lot to gain in Africa, but there is a lot to lose as well. An investment in good governance and rule of law will ultimately enhance the business climate that US companies need to have to expand business successfully all over Africa.

In the DRC and the Great Lakes, US commerce and corporations maintain huge interests in securing lucrative contracts, and the US pays handsomely for the UN's peacekeeping budget in the DRC—the only measure right now that is keeping DRC from disintegrating. However, Joseph Kabila and DRC require more governance mentoring by the US. American DRC policy, unclear to many, is often trumped by the guilty ridden relationship with neighboring Rwanda. But this unbalanced relationship has destabilized the DRC and also restricts the consolidation of US commercial and political power on the African continent, as other African countries watch and learn that the mouse (Rwanda) can blind the master (the US).

It is therefore critical for the US to ensure that Rwanda detaches completely from interference in the DRC. In this way, playing a more direct peacemaker role and mentoring governance in the DRC, would significantly contribute to stabilization of the entire continent.

While President Obama has scaled up action against LRA and Somali pirates, he has not initiated a strategic engagement with Africa, the Great Lakes and sub-Saharan Africa. The potential returns on political and governance engagement in Africa can be enormous as the continent moves to 6-8 per cent per annum economic growth rates, promising markets and resources in abundance. Africa is missing the political and governance culture to benefit from these gains as the US and others lose the opportunities to take advantage of Africa's economic boom.

Chapter 4

US Foreign Policy in Europe

"With the shifting focus to Asia-Pacific, Obama has made perhaps the most definitive change in US foreign policy since the declaration of the Marshall Plan"

Since the WWII years, the US relationship with Europe has been premised on guaranteeing global peace and security, and ensuring that a global conflict such as World War I and II will never comes to pass again.

This is a key relationship for the US in security cooperation and enforcement. US investment in NATO and in collaborative defensive postures with Western European countries first confronted the Soviet Union and the perceived menace posed by the encroaching control of Communism. This collaboration not only allowed for deep cooperation on defensive command and control strategy, but also on R&D in the arms sector leading to significant developments in the weapons industry both in the US and Europe.

The success of NATO to this day is premised on the mutual advantage that this defense mechanism bestows on its member states, and the cohesive defensive strategy. Military cohesiveness proved to be a critical byproduct of NATO, when it came to post-9/11 intelligence cooperation and the fight against al-Qaeda. Throughout the generations of European military and political leaders, their commitment to NATO has not waned, but with the advent of global terrorism and new security challenges such as cyber-terrorism, the mutual US-European commitment to use NATO as a coordinating mechanism for joint response, has been strengthened, not weakened.

A second significant aspect of the relationship centers on economic and industrial progress, including global free trade and R&D, which has always been amicably competitive. Banking and fast-evolving financial markets were a hallmark of the US Wall Street era but Europe was not far behind, adopting a more conservative yet steady approach.

CHALLENGES IN THE RELATIONSHIP

Two factors have challenged the density of the US-European relationship. Firstly, the success of the evolving European Union at a social, legal and economic level as increased intra-European cohesion in mainstreaming legal and government policy on such issues as immigration, freedom of movement and commercial/trading laws. This has bought European countries closer together and has also implied that mutual consultation on critical European and International issues at times trumped the imperatives of the relationship with the US.

Secondly, the fall of the Iron Curtain and the subsequent collapse of the Soviet Union removed the original impetus to hold commitment to NATO. Instead, a huge number of Eastern European countries rushed to join the EU, hoping to gain development assistance to upgrade their ailing social infrastructure and to get jobs and gain access to the high standard of living of Western Europe. This also paved the way for the reunification of Western and Eastern Germany, on the backs of Europe's "people power" that manually broke down the Berlin Wall. The net result was a boost to the economies and the industry of Europe as a whole, strengthening the efforts of the original nine Western European countries to create assured security through irreversible inter-dependence in all possible sectors.

Contrary to expectations, the process of opening up Eastern Europe and the diminishing threat from Communism actually strengthened the relationship of the US with a larger and more entrepreneurial Europe, expanding the pool of countries in the coalition of the willing that supported both the strengthening and consolidation of the EU and the expansion of NATO.

Fight against Terrorism: The events of 9/11 and the subsequent terrorist incidents in London and other European countries provided a significant basis for renewed collaboration, expanding intelligence cooperation and giving NATO and organizations such as Interpol, a new lease of life and purpose. Intelligence cooperation has reached a high since 9/11 in the US-European combined efforts to fight terrorism at its root.

While intelligence cooperation has many times contravened European human rights conventions and EU human rights laws, as well as national civil and human rights guarantees, it has nevertheless forged a new and definitive agenda for US-European collaboration and cohesion. Legal and human rights objections to the many transgressions of International and national laws, importantly to European nationals being held and investigated at *Guantanamo camp entre autre,* have been ignored and brushed aside to what is considered, the larger terrorism fighting agenda.

The Arab Spring: Yet another aspect of the evolution of US-European foreign policy congruence is the response to such ground swell processes as the Arab Spring. US, UK and France—who also constitute the Permanent 3 (P3) of the Permanent 5 (P5) nations of the Security Council—have been united in their response to the unfolding events the Arab Spring in Tunisia, Egypt, Yemen, Libya and now Syria and Bahrain, although the responses have not been equal for all scenarios. Not wanting to lose the relative stability of decades of political and security support to the entrenched dictatorships of Ben Ali, Mubarak and Saleh, the P3 countries tried to salvage relations after the Arab democratic revolutions seemed to have succeeded. US, UK and France faced a rising tide of opinion against the dubious legacy of their policies in the Middle East region.

At the heart of their response to Middle East grievances was the unmitigated commitment of the P3 to the continued consolidation of Israel over Palestinian lands and the commensurate decrease in the pressure applied by the P3 on Israel to stop settlement activity and to come to the negotiating table with the Palestinian side, around a two-state solution. Used to the French and the British as old colonial powers (see Map 4, page 70)[86] with a negative legacy on the Palestinian issue and on the dividing the former Baathist Iraq into post-WWII Iraq, Syria and Jordan, they perceived the US as a more powerful but malevolent influence. Over the decades, the

---

86   http://www.flickr.com/photos/normanbleventhalmapcenter/2710789398/

use of US's unmitigated economic and political power to keep the Middle East subjugated under the very tyrannical dictators that the Arab Spring succeeded in over throwing, and the economic and security consolidation of Israel, were two reasons why the P3 were hated yet feared throughout the Middle East.

MAP OF EUROPEAN COLONIZATION OF THE MIDDLE EAST (MAP 4)

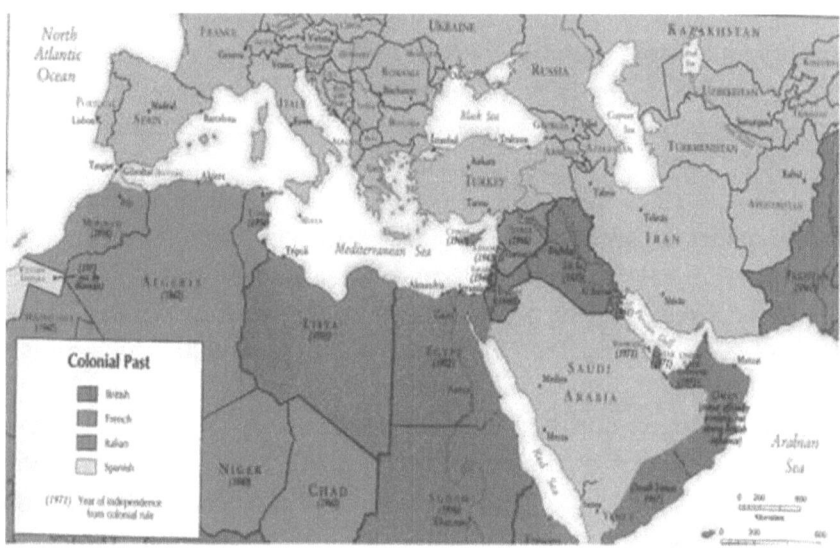

After the unification of Germany and the emergence of Germany as one of the strongest economies in the world and the most powerful in Europe, it has played a markedly independent role from UK and France, within the EU on foreign policy and vis-à-vis the US in its foreign and strategic initiatives. Germany has led a number of European countries in moving away from blanket support of US policy recommendations, and in a number of cases—Syria, Libya, Sri Lanka and between Israel and Palestine—served as mediator. This role has evolved due to the non-militarized nature of Germany, and because they have had a very deep and well considered foreign policy. Not hesitating to disagree with Franco-British constructs on emerging foreign policy issues where the US has taken a lead to posit a line of action.

German media, much more independent and critical, is a source of truth for many in Europe and Eastern Europe, and has often exposed the superficiality and "policy-based" nature of US news reporting. These trends, while not pursued aggressively by either party, point to the concrete fact that many European countries do not fall as neatly behind the US on foreign policy issues and strategic policy as the UK and France tend to do. My analysis indicates that divergences on key policy and security initiatives might start to widen in the coming months and years, as cases such as Syria and Iran, elicit heterogeneous approaches and understandings.

NATO's Action in Libya: Falling Dominoes and Disruption

For three decades, NATO engaged limited active military campaigns, instead prioritizing command systems and force training in the state-of-the-art warfare techniques. This evolution paralleled the development of European based arms industries that competed with the giant US defense industries.

Under pressure from the US, UK and France (the P3), the UN Security Council passed a resolution requesting NATO[87] to help to enforce a no-fly zone over strategic areas of Libya, thereby giving the Libyan rebels a level playing field from which to fight the incumbent Gaddafi regime. There was also significant military support handed over in the form of arms, ammunition, communications equipment, as well as, humanitarian and medical assistance.

The NATO role was limited to the maintenance of an air cordon but the challenge that was to emerge in Libya was much larger and much more significant. Even before Gaddafi was killed, large sections of his army started to migrate out of the country with huge stashes of weapons and ammunition, something that was reported on by media but not acted upon by the US, UK and France. Containing the spread of these

---

[87]   http://www.nato.int/cps/en/SID-5F2418B423EC9324/natolive/news_75177.htm
http://www.nato.int/cps/en/SID-5F2418B423EC9324/natolive/official_texts_72544.htm

arms within Libya and outside Libya to the region was de-emphasized by NATO, because NATO was not prepared to commit troops. Regardless whether this was a slip by the UN, or by the P3 that had orchestrated much of the Libyan liberation, the fact is that the arms and ammunition smuggled out of Libya, subsequently triggered a series of events further south in West Africa.

In Mali, Al-Qaeda has succeeded in establishing an independent state, and in Northern Nigeria, fundamentalist groups linked to Al-Qaeda are securing access to Libyan arms with the objective of declaring independence from Nigeria. Other West African states such as Liberia and Cote D'Ivoire that are facing a more tenuous phase in their bid to irreversibly consolidate the rule of law and stability, will also likely face fallout as caches of Libyan weapons are now easily available on the market at low prices. The specter of the post-WWII *dominoes theory* has been realized in the unlikely scenario of Libya and West Africa, as a result of the unchecked mayhem of the Libyan revolution.

More serious however, is the fact that the US did not engage directly with the new Libyan regime by mentoring and supporting the fledgling government in rebuilding critical security and governance capacities that had been lost in the exodus of the Gaddafi regime. The gap in engagement with post-Gaddafi Libya defined the detached approach of the Obama administration on Libya and constituted a continuation of their policy to defer policy leadership in the Middle East increasingly to their European partners. This might have contributed directly to the incidents that led on 9/11/2012 to the fatal attacks that claimed the lives of four Americans in Benghazi, including Ambassador Christopher Stevens.

FUTURE OF THE ARAB SPRING AND IRAN

After Egypt and Libya, the US-UK-France coalition looked more cohesive and united than ever before in its bid to consolidate a new security regiment. The current revolution in Syria and the marshaling of international sanctions against Iran *(see analysis on Iran, page 20)* is a natural follow-up to what is emerging as the new "divide and rule" strategy for the Middle East, particularly as the US starts to refocus its attention to the Asia-Pacific as its most important zone of operation.

Acting together and pushing for global action against Iran has given the P3 led by the US a new zero-sum game with which to classify the 196 countries of the world as friends or not-so-friendly. But it has also raised many questions about the double standards applied by the US, UK and France towards a nuclear-armed Israel versus a nuclear-energy proficient Iran.

There is little doubt amongst analysts that this hypocrisy extends to the nascent struggle of the people of Bahrain to gain more representation and a stronger voice in their own governance *(see analysis on Bahrain, page 13)*. Far from over, the Bahrain war hinges on the historic US and UK military support to the corrupt rulers of that small country. Cases such as Bahrain reconfirm that the US, UK and France as key members of a Security Council that is meant to safe-guard the world against war, are at times complicit in perpetuating global insecurity and instability directly through their client relationships.

In the case of Iran, the latest IAEA report on the status of the Iran nuclear program glosses over the fact that Iran remains within the limits of its declared objectives of nuclear energy for civilian use. While the US has said that it has no evidence that Iran is conclusively moving towards nuclear weapons proficiency, many questions arise in countries observing the process, that are looking for facts instead of assumptions to maintain the credibility and impartiality of the current Japanese IAEA leadership.

CHANGING FOCUS OF THE US

On 6 January 2012, President Obama announced new priorities in US Foreign Policy focused on building up key partnerships in the Asia-Pacific[88]. This was greeted with caution in the region itself as countries like India, Indonesia and Malaysia, are more circumspect in their approach to the US after the Arab Spring. They might not make public announcements on

---

[88] http://www.bostonglobe.com/news/nation/2012/01/06/obama-outlines-new-military-strategy-focusing-asia-pacific-region-and-middle-east/bwYBkrOn6fyjzvWJliujWO/story.html
http://www.defense.gov/news/newsarticle.aspx?id=66706

their dislike of the content and implementation of some US foreign policy but their disdain is barely masked.

While a majority of Pacific countries seek to engage in trade and international economics with the US, there is a discernible move away from subscribing to or supporting, US global policy. As Asia-Pacific countries have learnt lessons from the US misadventures in the Middle East and will not seek to replicate those, as the US turns to focus its attention on their region.

Europe, with lingering legacies of its colonial history in the Asia-Pacific is also cautious, knowing better than most, the high moral stance of the independent politicians of Asia. Obama's announcement that the US is a Pacific nation have, to some extent, alarmed Europeans, who have spent 200 years relating to the US as an Atlantic nation.

The US-European relationship and the US commitment to Europe remain strong. International trade, financial resurgence and banking, as well as security coordination through NATO and on intelligence cooperation in the fight against terrorism have led to increasing cohesion. It remains to be seen how the rest of Europe, Germany, Belgium, Spain, Italy and others will now approach its relations with the US on key international events and processes such as Syria, Iran and Bahrain.

The German, Dutch and other European medias are much more objective and much more critical when reporting on the Middle East, presenting analysis that often challenges US media and government pronouncements. Most importantly, other parts of Europe are less inclined to join the coalition of the US, UK and France, and support instead, a more balanced world power picture. Time will tell whether the crisis in the Eurozone will exacerbate or diminish the rising debate in Europe about US foreign policy in the world.

Chapter 5

US, Russia and China: Shifting Balances

> "*. . . the failure of the international community to unite in action in the Security Council has not only spotlighted the consolidation of the P3 (US, UK, France), but also the diplomatic re-emergence of Russia and China.*"

The most striking image to emerge from the June 2012 G20 meeting in Mexico was of Russian President Putin consulting with Chinese President Hua. Putin's demeanor is full of respect and is almost deferential to his Chinese counterpart, who seems to be listening with attention. Russia and China are now in the process of cooperating, coordinating and strategizing on how to contain their common adversary, the United States.

There are many reasons why in 2012, China and Russia have cause to be each other's best friend. The most significant being *economic* rapprochement—both countries have more to gain from economic cooperation with each other than with any other country or region—and the *strategic* need to balance the growing global dominance of the US. The two perceive that they have much to lose by the damage that the US can wreak on their individual and combined global interest.

As the US pushes hard through the UN and other international mechanisms to enforce its policy stance on Israel-Palestine and Syria—for example, on 19 July in the UN Security Council Russia and China vetoed a UK-drafted resolution on Syria for an "10 day ultimatum" to the Assad regime—Russia and China are compelled to err on the side of caution concerning pre-emptive military action *a la* Libya. They also have an interest in making others question the wisdom of US's cowboy antics in the world today. The broader ramifications of the perception of US international politics was well illustrated by the decisions of Pakistan and South Africa to absent from the same 19 July vote.

RUSSIA AND CHINA

> *"Bullying Russia (and China) will only result in stonewalling by the Kremlin and worse, blocking by Russia of worthy initiatives in the international arena. It is in no one's interest to return to a Cold War political stance."*

Russia's relation with China, a neighboring country that has shared an ideology but has approached its implementation on a different trajectory, has not been one of a traditional friend or collaborator until now.

There are certainly a lot of complementarities between China and Russia that would allow a flourishing mutuality. China has a huge dependence on oil, while Russia is a major oil exporter; China has prospered from a cutting edge production economy and corners the market on work and business ethic when it comes to cheap and chic. Russian industry is outmoded and its infrastructure is struggling to keep up.

Low-level investment in industry and infrastructure have left Russia far behind the Asia-Pacific and the US. Its share of the global arms trade has been declining (*see data presented in the Introduction*). This means that Russian and Eastern European weapons and small arms industries have to explore new markets for small arms and light or medium-range weapons that can take on armored military units. Other Russian products like medicines and medical equipment also face marked demand from non-traditional producers. Russia has to upgrade and modernize its aging industrial and light manufacturing capacity to turn over its economy, and therefore requires some demand for present production to help finance the transition. The emergent Middle East could absorb some of this light industrial production, especially if suspicion and distrust of the US continues to grow, but only if Russia quickly moderates its policy on Syria to contain Arab animosity.

Putin needs to balance and finance the aspirations of the young Russians who elected him and who expect jobs, growth and glory. New markets for arms and light industry could provide the answer.

The Chinese economy records over 7 per cent growth every year except for presently. Even lower 2012 levels remain well above those recorded in the West. Russia could learn and emulate some of these successes on the technological side, although even more interesting for Russia is the Chinese entrepreneurial model. Both nations have poor and undeveloped rural populations. Given the large scale of both countries, solutions could be shared in order to optimize social rehabilitation. Lastly, both share highly centralized economies in which decision-making on a host of economic and internal/external security policy issues are interlinked and taken at the leadership level.

These constraints imply that only China and Russia would be able to understand and advise each other on their internal economic rehabilitative processes. In foreign policy, the hegemonic attitude and leadership of the US has given China and Russia reason to cooperate and realize their common interests above erstwhile competitive ones. Both China and Russia are also ostracized by the US and the West for human rights transgressions against their own populations and against neighboring states or territories.

Recent muscle flexing in the UN Security Council responds to Russia and China's basic foreign policy instincts and interests. Firstly, Russia desires to regain its Cold War position of power and respect in the global arena, looking to challenge and balance the power of the US and allies France and the UK. Secondly, Russia has lost friends and client states in Eastern Europe and Caucasus since the fall of the Berlin Wall; Syria and Iran now constitute the remaining two adherents in the Middle East. Russia and China will not abandon them, contrary to a practice often ascribed to the US of acting on a short-term policy vision.

China also feels that the changes bought on by the Arab Spring have manifested with unnatural speed and decisiveness. Syria and particularly Iran are client states and allies that need to be supported. China also fears the example that the Arab Spring sets for its own very restive Western and Southern populations, where Muslim Chinese populations and other minorities are in a latent but not inactive long term resistance against Beijing. Libya was a step too far and is now regretted by both Russia and China.

While definitely enjoying a privileged relationship with Iran, China does not care so much for Syria as for blocking international action out of fear of encouraging rebellion at home. Like Russia, China is allergic to the Obama administration's policy mantra of *regime change.*

RUSSIA

> *"Putin needs to balance and finance the aspirations of the young Russians who elected him and who expect jobs, growth and glory. New markets for arms and light industry could provide the answer."*

The national political and media discourse surrounding Putin's presidency has been wary of his appeal as a powerful and dynamic global figure, a nationalist who has prioritized the return of the power and prestige of Mother Russia.

Domestic Constituency Spells Challenges

The truth is that Putin's brand of grandiose nationalism appeals to a significant majority of the Russian electorate, who need to believe that everyday life and opportunities will magically multiply and are accessible. Their belief is partially premised on the lack of any other viable political vision on the horizon. Simply put: Putin's vision for a return of the glory of Mother Russia is the best grade of opium available to the frustrated masses in Russia.

Putin's effective power would not have been so strong if he had not effectively decimated his political and popular (media; human rights; civil rights groups) opposition by manufacturing elaborate corporate and tax fraud vendettas against them, or simply arresting and harassing them via his growing network of public goons. Equally, any sign of budding leadership qualities among party cadres has been squashed. Corruption is rife[89]. Western media has picked up on reports of Putin's Versailles on the banks of the Black sea, a palace worthy of Neptune.

Putin's leadership is fast creating a hybrid society in Russia. Investigations reveal that Government contracts worth millions and billions, lucrative purchasing orders, state posts, governorships and posts in state-run corporate structures are being designated by Putin's nomination. His friends, their families and a group of ex-KGB and Russian Army officers[90] are being chosen to fill orders and take over ceremonial roles that give them key control over local and national corporate and legal structures. They have the power and prerogative to initiate legal changes and rezoning of districts in key zones in Russia and around its major industrial and urban areas.

Putin's agenda so far only promises to further polarize, divide and instrumentalize the Russian economy and workforce. High oil prices are providing temporary relief to the economy, but may not last long. Starting in 2013, Russia will face dire economic challenges that could have security implications for all of us.

Russian Foreign Policy: US and China

With Libya as a living example of the consequences of the Arab Spring, Putin has maintained a firm line on Syria, even if the policy now seems more harmful than helpful in Putin's quest to reestablish Russian global power. Putin's Foreign Minister Sergei Lavrov has threatened to use the Security Council veto to prevent any Security Council resolution on military intervention in Syria. Further, he is defending the right of Russia and its surrogates to trade weapons, ammunition and intelligence with Syria and other countries.

Russia is also criticizing the sanctions on Iran proposed by Washington as aimed solely at the Iranian people to "incite" popular revolution against

---

[89] http://www.economist.com/blogs/easternapproaches/2012/03/putins-return?bclid=0&bctid=1485530842001

[90] http://www.aljazeera.com/news/europe/2012/03/201231665525590255.html#.UD-duPuKXn0.gmail

the Government[91]. To prove his point, Putin has accused the new US ambassador to Russia of supporting the Russian political opposition. Whatever the reality of the charges, Putin is evidencing his of political revolution in Russia reminiscent of the Arab Spring.

Putin's new *Mother Russia* foreign policy stance could have ramifications beyond the Near and Middle East. Most of Europe's gas supply comes from Russia, and this dependence could provide leverage on the European Union. Secondly, by threatening to use the Security Council veto, there is a danger that the importance and centrality of the Security Council is marginalized vis-à-vis Syria and Iran. While this would not be the first time that the US has led a reluctant alliance into battle, it also harks back to the era of the Cold War when the UN and the Security Council were largely deadlocked.

In this context, it is interesting that on 21 June 2012, Henry Kissinger met privately with Putin in St Petersburg[92]. This "track-two" initiative is seen as an essential step in using a tried and tested diplomacy tools to moderate the evolving clash with Russia (and China and others) on the Iran nuclear issue. The meeting has the blessings of the US State Department, cognizant that Kissinger may be an old-time diplomat but he is a Russia expert and a supreme strategist, respected by Putin.

In Putin's favor is growing unease regarding the US and its two main allies, the UK and France. There is growing trepidation of pre-emptive US policy, meaning that, today more than yesterday, countries are willing to consider new and innovative global partnerships that maintain the sanctity of sovereignty and of international diplomacy as paramount. Whether Russia will be able to cast its politics in a frame to be able to take advantage of this opening is not clear. If yes, it could deliver to Russia the allies and power it seeks to re-create, if only in antithesis to the US.

---

[91] http://rt.com/politics/russia-iran-sanctions-un-cooperation-us-268/

[92] http://english.ruvr.ru/2012_06_21/78879876/

Conclusions

Russia under Putin is at a crossroads. If Putin persists in dictatorial and nepotistic leadership, Russia will not be able to take on its national challenges. If he moves toward more enlightened leadership and a dexterous Russia, Russia in the near future has the potential to re-emerge as a global power.

Russia is watching the coming elections in the US with trepidation. One of the key concerns is the US-proposed European missile defense system. According to Putin, he would have much more confidence that he could reach an agreement with President Obama[93] then with Republican candidate Mitt Romney. This is a direct allusion to Romney's comments that Russia remains the number 1 enemy of the US. The future of the relationship depends to a large extent on the mutual foreign policy approach and President Obama represent the more attractive option.

US foreign policy towards Russia has to be open-ended and non-prescriptive. It has to be based on formality and respect for a Russian nation of consequence in the world. Bullying Russia will only result in stonewalling by the Kremlin and worse, blocking by Russia of worthy initiatives in the international arena. It is in no one's interest to return to a Cold War political stance.

The US needs to re-engage Russia experts who support a "dovish" mentality and seek to reestablish a working *détente*. Any other course of action will freeze international and multilateral fora and consolidate the image of a US seeking to monopolize international leadership. The Obama administration has not adopted a new stance on Russia, but has let old policies linger. Lack of engagement could be ascribed to caution, but more likely should be appreciated as a lack of a truly strategic approach.

---

[93] http://www.nytimes.com/2012/09/07/world/europe/putin-calls-missile-deal-more-likely-if-obama-wins.html

CHINA

"China holds huge US dollar and US government securities reserves, and disposing of even 4 per cent of its reserves could be disastrous for the US economy[94] in terms of higher borrowing costs"

After the introversion of the Cultural Revolution, China has been steadily building its power and position as a regional if not a global mega power. During the Cold War, China did not shrink from taking on the then-more powerful US by supporting armed Communist insurgencies in Vietnam, Cambodia, Korea and other countries. However, with a burgeoning population, China embarked on a steep march to industrialization.

Since the 1970s China has consolidated its industrialization revolution, taking millions of people out of poverty. China has also emerged as a powerhouse in its accumulation of dollar and euro reserves and business outreach in Africa and Latin America. Today, China not the US is the most sought after trading and development partner among any lesser-developed milieu, simply because the Chinese do not attach moral judgements or impose conditionalities on, trade and development relationships.

But all has not gone smoothly for China in its own backyard. The US has maintained a strong political and military foothold in the Philippines, South Korea and Japan (*see Map 5*), as a means of balancing China's growing regionalism. The US has prioritized its relationships in the Asia-Pacific, calling itself a "Pacific" power. Changes in loyalties in South and Pacific Asia have been observable in the shifting alliances and alliance contexts between US-Pakistan, US-India, and China-India-Pakistan on the one hand, and between China-Philippines-Malaysia-Vietnam-Myanmar on the other. A double or treble balancing act is further complicated by the economic and social resurgence in Indonesia and Malaysia, who after decades under authoritarian rule have emerged as strong third-tier economic and political powers. At the same time they are establishing a more centrist, independent foreign policy stance vis-à-vis the two jostling mega powers.

---

[94]   http://www.fas.org/sgp/crs/row/RL34314.pdf

MAP OF US DEPLOYMENTS IN THE ASIA-PACIFIC REGION (MAP 5)

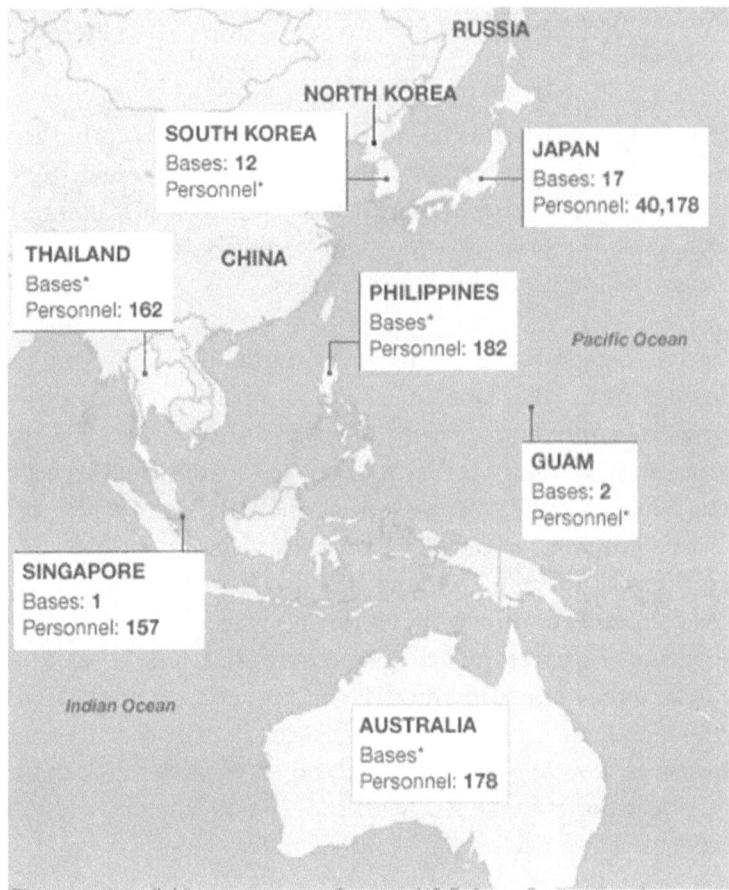

China is an economic miracle that needs to keep growing, building, adapting and absorbing to maintain its 7 per cent-plus annual GDP growth. Unlike Russia, China is in a very strong position, holding the largest amount of US dollar foreign currency reserves in the world, even more than the US itself, estimated at some 70 per cent of the total global deposit. China has a much more aggressive and exploratory foreign policy than Russia, allowing it to build relationships with a host of nations not immediately in its natural sphere of influence. It has a calm foreign policy demeanor, allowing even "naughty" states financial aid and support so long as access to natural resources is unfettered.

China needs to maintain or transmute its economic miracle to encompass its rural populations and to sustain this transformation for another two decades before it is ready to take over the leadership of the world. More than the US or Russia, it is in a position to emerge as a global leader in the next two decades if it can maintain economic growth.

China's strategy in Africa has been successfully built on securing access to lucrative oil, mineral and natural resource contracts. In exchange, China is building infrastructure (government and Parliamentary structure, roads, hospitals, prisons, social housing) and giving development assistance without any political or rights-based linkages.

For the last decade, China's African expansion was criticized for not adding value to the development objectives of the target countries, but of simply delivering what appeared to be large public works and physical infrastructure in exchange for resources. A lesser-advertised aspect of the Chinese contribution was training and education in a host of technical areas like engineering, medicine, communications and media[95]. In 2012, Chinese Central TV (CCTV) launched its network in Africa, covering the whole continent, employing and being managed by African media personnel and journalists trained and educated in China[96]. While adding a new style to the routine commercial and development programs offered by traditional donor countries, CCTV Africa actually contributes to the continent-wide flow of information and employment, building confidence among African professionals who work shoulder-to-shoulder with Chinese colleagues to deliver news and TV programming.

Internationally and politically, China is more pragmatic than Russia. It nevertheless cannot be pushed around by a US on its human rights record, and on liberalization of trade regulations and floating currencies. Such liberalization would require a considerable legal, financial and infrastructural adjustment. China holds huge US dollar and US government

---

[95] http://english.gov.cn/official/2010-12/23/content_1771603_6.htm
[96] http://allafrica.com/stories/201201160075.html

securities reserves, and disposing of even 4 per cent of its reserves could be disastrous for the US economy[97] in terms of higher borrowing costs[98].

China has embarked on a fast-track professionalization and transformation of its military and naval capacity, announcing a huge budget for R&D and weapons development. They are planning to triple their current naval strength at the cutting edge of technology. One explanation for the US re-focusing on the Pacific as a policy priority is apprehension about China's strengthening naval capacities. Under the President's personal leadership, the US announced significant new military cooperation in the region, including agreements with Australia and boots-on-the-ground in that country and others in the Pacific Rim. The US has also announced a concentration of naval forces in Asia-Pacific over the next decade. This in turn is perceived by China as a challenge to China's most important sphere of influence, the Asia-Pacific, and a direct challenge by the US on naval capacity[99].

US-CHINA-INDIA-PAKISTAN

The 1972 meeting between Richard Nixon, Henry Kissinger and the Chinese leadership in Beijing was organized by Pakistan, and marked a definitive peak in the cordiality of relations between Pakistan and the US. Since then, US-Chinese relations have hee-hawed or waxed and waned, responsive to global events and regional opportunities in the Asia-Pacific to promote and further, US or Chinese spheres of influence. Cambodia, Korea, Vietnam and countless other mini-confrontations later during the Cold War, US-Chinese relations have been strengthened in the last decade due to the rising economic power of China.

By contrast during decades, India was militarily and ideologically supported by the Soviet Union. A closed country, the US perception of India was shaped for decades by India's conflict with Pakistan and their

---

[97]   http://www.fas.org/sgp/crs/row/RL34314.pdf
[98]   http://online.wsj.com/article/SB10001424052970203753704577254794068655760.html
[99]   http://www.foreignaffairs.com/articles/138009/andrew-j-nathan-and-andrew-scobell/how-china-sees-america

closeness with Soviet Union. Episodes such as the Union Carbine disaster led to a very weary relationship between India and the US, up till India declared publicly their Soviet-supported nuclear status in the late 1970's. Then the US realized that the second most populous country in the world had huge potential and implications, both as an ally or a foe. Since then, India has been prompted to open up its economy and its industry to global competition by its intellectually dexterous manpower, turning the tables on Pakistan and the US.

India today, is a force to be recognized militarily, intellectually and as a potential global power. Meanwhile, long-festering border disputes in Nepal, Tibet and Sikkim have often pitted India against China, and India has actively maintained a balance of power posture in the Bay of Bengal.

With the successful testing of Agni 5 in April 2012, India has launched itself into a more exclusive nuclear club then its neighbor and rival Pakistan, into the intermediate range missile club. Coupled with its nuclear submarine capacity, India could be perceived as moving from a policy of balancing China to an active policy of containment. It seems logical that one of the considerations that drove the Chinese decision to upgrade its naval fleet is the much superior naval capacity of India, now perceived by China as a regional competitor militarily. If this assessment is correct, then India is indirectly indicating its willingness to play a containment role further then the Bay of Bengal and even the Indian Ocean. It is worthy of note that India tested the 50 ton, 51 foot Agni 5 with the full knowledge and blessing of the US, who issued official statements attesting to India's nuclear safety record. It can be inferred that the US has blessed India's expanded new role of containment vis-à-vis China, perhaps as far as the Asia-Pacific.

In September 2012, an announcement of joint military and naval exercises between India and China has surprised the US; this illustrates India's commitment to maintain an independent and deeply strategic policy posture internationally, and not necessarily in favor of or in line with US plans. This initiative underscores the more mediatory nature of conflict resolution through statesmanship in Asia-Pacific as compared the more reactive militaristic nature of US policy.

At the same time, US relations with Pakistan are in a steep downward slide. The decline has resulted in a changed power balance for China, who used the growing discord between Pakistan and US to secure access to Gwadar, a Pakistani port that they are going to construct on the Arabia Gulf. While a realigned balance of power in that sub-region might be US-India and China-Pakistan, giving the Bay of Bengal, Indian Ocean and the Pacific Basin a new power hierarchy, Relations between India and China may yet consolidate along constructive lines.

Asia-Pacific and East Asia: the Crouching Tigers

The biggest change in economic and political power and diplomatic impact over the last 15 years has occurred in East Asia. The countries referred to as the Asian Tigers are the Philippines, Malaysia, Indonesia and South Korea (G7 and recent OECD member). Potentially to follow are Vietnam, Thailand, Myanmar and Cambodia.

Malaysia and Indonesia have achieved the most amazing turnarounds politically, emerging from decades of stifling and brutal dictatorships, to rise up in economic might built on sheer hard work and in the case of Malaysia, oil revenues. So magnificent and notable has been their ascent and so solid successive decades of high economic growth rates that Indonesia is being talked about in the same league as India, a charter BRIC member (Brazil; Russia; India; China).

Their economic power has not led to more regional influence although Malaysia is a major sponge for Asian talent and attracts streams of migrant labor. We see that Malaysia and Indonesia yield easily to the US demand to stop trading or cooperating with Iran by significantly reducing their trade and technical exchange with that country on industrial issues. This is in marked contrast to India, which negotiated an alternative payment scheme with Iran rather than manage without their petroleum. This implies that the Asian Tigers have prioritized economic development and social development over becoming a regional or global power.

THE SOUTH CHINA SEA

"China has a much more aggressive and exploratory foreign policy than Russia, allowing it to build relationships with a host of nations not immediately in its natural sphere of influence."

MAP OF THE SOUTH CHINA SEA (MAP 6)[100]

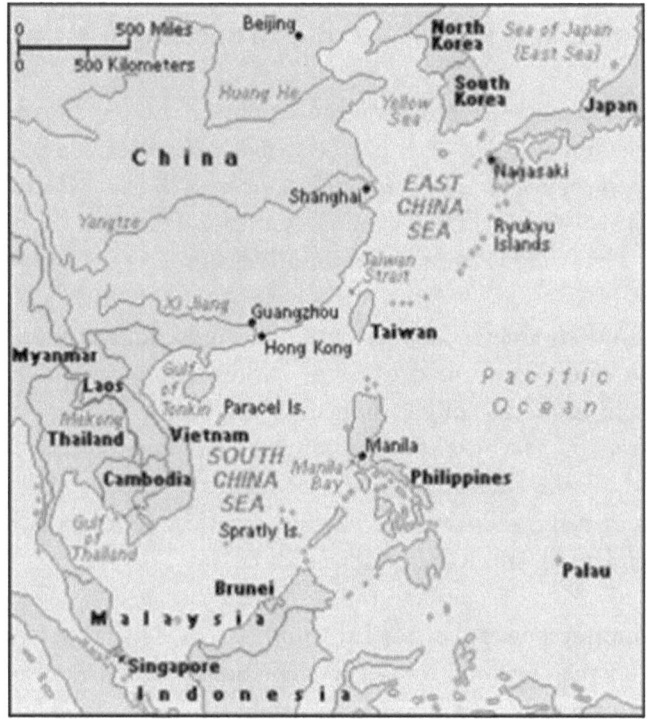

Challenges arise for China when sharing the South China Sea with the Philippines, Japan, Vietnam, Thailand and Cambodia. The region of the South China Sea constitutes a very important shipping and transport passage for most of Asia-Pacific but also, is thought to contain lucrative oil and gas reserves that are currently unexploited due to the contested ownership of the waters. The attraction is not only black gold like oil and gas, it is also about lucrative fishing waters, corals, exotic and endangered

---

[100] http://geography.howstuffworks.com/oceans-and-seas/the-china-sea.htm

ocean life-like giant scallops and clams. All the seafood and aquatic treasures that the Chines and the Japanese value as delicacies can be found in these waters. There are regular reports of clashes and ocean maneuvers involving any one of the six or seven claimant countries.

Most at stake are the Spratly Islands, a group of more than 750 islands, atolls, reefs and islets that form an archipelago off the coast of Philippines, Malaysia and Vietnam. They contain less than four square kilometers of land area spread over more than 425,000 square kilometers of sea. This complicates governance and economics in that region of Southeast Asia. While these small and remote islands have little economic value in themselves, they are important in establishing international boundaries. There are no native islanders but there are, at least for now, rich fishing grounds; and initial surveys indicate the islands may contain significant reserves of oil and natural gas.

MAP OF THE SPRATLY ISLANDS (MAP7)

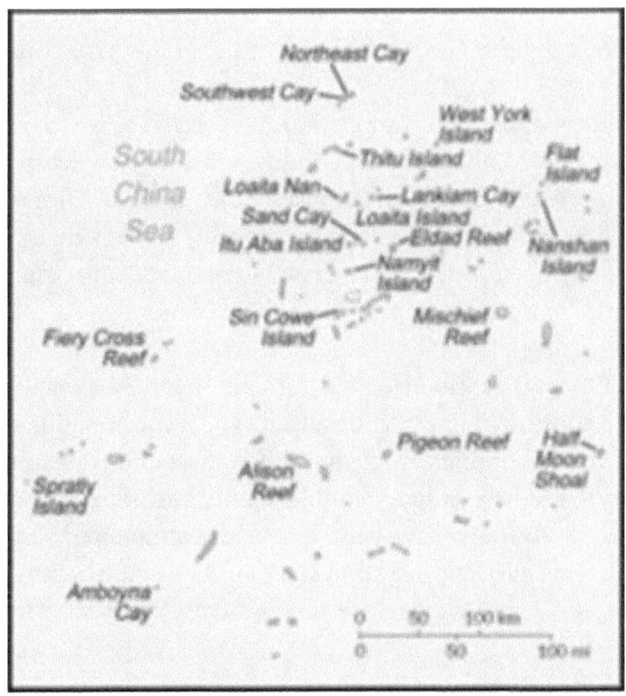

What is most interesting is that China perhaps does not covert the islands themselves as much as the oil and gas reserves that are rumored to lie on the ocean floor. This has been illustrated in the competing claims by China and Japan concerning five uninhabited islands called Senkaku in Japan and Diaoyu in China; the islands reportedly were occupied by Japan as part of their imperialist expansion in 1895 but were originally Chinese. At issue are the oil reserves at the bed of the islands. China wishes to start exploration to meet its ever-growing demand for crude oil but it cannot do so until the others drop their claims to the islands.

China perceives that the South China Sea is being instrumentalized by the US and its surrogates in the Asia-Pacific region to thwart China's historic possession of what is naturally theirs. In September 2012, Secretary-of-State Hillary Clinton spent three days discussing the South China Sea and other issues in Beijing; the talks produced little more then the confirmation from top Chinese officials that they do not perceive any role for the US in the South China Sea and will absolutely resist US intervention in this affair[101]. Yet every month sees a slight escalation in the incidents and recriminations between the countries that share these waters and could be a divisive factor within the ASEAN group of countries.

On the military dimension, Indonesia and Malaysia as well as Philippines possess impressive and profession military forces and have benefitted from a growing and positive relationship with the US Military but also with the Chinese. Yet over the last few months, not less than five official statements have been issued by the State Department concerning the right of Philippines to a certain part of the Spratly islands.

President Obama's announcement of the new Asia-Pacific strategy amounted a confirmation of Chinese fears, and a confirmation of the shift of focus of the US military from the Middle East and Afghanistan to the Pacific. Naval and new military commitments, including plans to open a military base in Australia have been agreed and announced, indicating an expanded US military and naval presence in the Pacific basin. China sees

---

[101] http://abcnews.go.com/International/wireStory/clintons-china-visit-produces-breakthrough-17156826#.UEjzTkKhBFI

US expansion in the Asia-Pacific as a direct challenge of encirclement, and is probably is now considering its strategic response.

AUSTRALIA

A major economy in the periphery of the Asia-Pacific, Australia has steadily consolidated its military and strategic capacity since WWII. It now dominates the South Pacific and contributes to international initiatives led by the US such as the campaign in Afghanistan[102].

In 2011, US and Australia announced a scaling up of their military cooperation, with the US deploying military and navy personnel to new US bases in Australia[103]. The objective clearly is to contain what is perceived as a Chinese bid to modernize and expand their navy, thereby also expanding the scope of their influence in the Northern Pacific and South Asia.

Constituting a key facet of the emerging new US Pacific strategy, the expansion of bases in Australia is a bold move, taking place at a time of belt tightening and fiscal cuts for the US, It signals the Obama Administration's strong commitment to the US role in the Pacific. However, 2012 being an election year raises some questions about the commitment behind this strategy after November. With all the budget cuts promised as part of the republican campaign, a leadership transition would probably would have implication for the continuity and depth of US's new Pacific strategy.

Conclusions

China remains the most dynamic yet surprising country in the world today. It has the potential to produce and share many perhaps thousands of miracles with the rest of the world over the next decades, drawing on the talents and sheer numerical strength of its burgeoning youth population. Unfortunately, it also has the potential to spin out of control, being unable

---

102 http://www.quarterlyessay.com/issue/time-war-australia-military-power
103 http://www.voanews.com/content/us-australia-announce-expanded-military-cooperation-133955288/148258.html

to "harness" the mounting economic, social and political aspirations of its population.

More US pressure in the Asia-Pacific will elicit an increasing cautious but direct response from China, including militarily. Mounting demographic and economic pressure inside China and the need to replicate the economic miracles of the last decade will push China to greater lengths. A potential clash can be anticipated if the emerging China-India naval cooperation fails, and afterwards India continues to push its regional leadership from the Bay of Bengal and Indian Ocean towards the South China Sea.

Yet this does mark a success for the US policy of containing China. By pinching and pushing from the South through India and from the East and South through the Asia-Pacific countries and the Tigers, the US has effectively encircled China and cordoned its influence to a limited seascape along its own coastline. Only time will tell if it is wise to push China into a defensive response posture, given that China holds sufficient US government treasury debt that it could use as an economic weapon.

Chapter 6

Concluding Analysis

President Obama had a mixed start after he was awarded the Nobel peace prize in 2009. His term in office heralded pronounced action in the realm of foreign policy and military strategic leadership globally, particularly in the Middle and Near East.

Foreign policy in which President Obama has been involved personally has made a direct contribution to US global power and has been a resounding success. These measures include the signing of nuclear reduction agreements and additional verification protocols with Russia, the full withdrawal from Iraq in 2011, and the signing of a Strategic Partnership Agreement with Afghanistan in May 2012. These initiatives constitute hallmarks of Obama foreign policy that were well received the international community, was supported by US allies, and responded to the clarion call of the American people to bring their sons home out of harm's way.

While endgames in Iraq and Afghanistan are vital foreign policy objectives, by far Obama's most important contribution to US foreign policy is his decision to shift US strategic focus to the Asia-Pacific. This new focus has far-reaching implications for US strategic policy, and implies a redrawing of the map in terms of the future US foreign policy, military power and development and social assistance. Practically, it implies that US Fifth Fleet based in Bahrain and US air force based in Saudi Arabia will probably constitute the Western-most deployment of significant US armed forces.

Military cooperation and bases in Asia, Asia-Pacific and Australia[104] will now take on a much more tailored, targeted and multi-disciplinary role. It also underscores that in coming decades, countries in the Asia-Pacific, China and the South China Sea[105]will receive more attention from Washington and the Pentagon than ever before. This policy refocus also has implications for potential future terms of reference for NATO, which could be more active in watching over the region west of Bahrain and Saudi Arabia, with Turkey as a pivotal Eastern-most member, while the overall leadership is retained by the US.

In perhaps his single biggest achievement, and one that shares glory with the foundation work laid down by President George W. Bush, President Obama "got" Osama Bin Laden.

Operation Geronimo that eliminated Osama Bin Laden was undertaken without consultation and to the detriment of the US relationship with Pakistan, a state that is failing and retains a lethal and virulent nuclear weapons arsenal, in a political and social milieu that is increasingly Islamic and fundamentalist. The destabilization of this relationship might bear heavy costs in the future.

Yet far from promoting calm and increasing a sense of security and peace, the strategic policy trajectory of the Obama Presidency has left a growing sense of discomfort with and distrust in US intentions among the 150 or so countries outside North America and Europe.

The growing unease can be attributed in part to the scaling up of drone warfare technology. Huge investments in drone technology have meant that the US is today capable of poisoning someone's coffee without them noticing. Miniature drones the size of mosquitoes, are being produced at various Air Force and CIA laboratories around the county[106]. This has also meant that the US is now capable of undertaking attacks, targeted

---

104   http://www.voanews.com/content/us-australia-agree-to-military-force-deployment-133946093/148236.html

105   http://www.nytimes.com/2012/04/05/world/asia/us-marines-arrive-darwin-australia.html

106   http://nhne-pulse.org/military-surveillance-swarms-of-cyborg-insects/

assassinations and spying missions without any human agent deployed in the field. Pakistan has borne the brunt of drone attacks over the last two years, and a number of key terrorist leaders have been assassinated using drones. Technological warfare, as it has come to be called, or nano-biotic technology, has changed the face of warfare on President Obama's watch.

A second cause for concern was the news that President Obama officially sanctioned increasing cyber warfare and virus attacks on Iran's nuclear program, at a time when the P5+1 (US, UK, France, Russia, China and Germany) were meeting with Iranian nuclear negotiators, and stringent financial and economic sanctions were about to go into effect against Iran[107]. This created an aura of distrust around the sincerity of the US and its president; it alienated Iran and effectively preempted the potential success of any negotiated solution. While many domestically applauded the President, others domestically and internationally were alarmed at the potential for the cyber viruses to cause the nuclear centrifuges to malfunction and emit radioactivity[108].

Germany felt deceived and finally not part of the 'team" (which was back to the original P3: US, UK, France), underscoring the lack of unity within the European Union on policy approaches and options to US led initiatives. In the post-Arab-Spring era, Europe is more circumspect about US foreign policy.

Contrary to expectations, President Obama has not invested in human rights considerations in forging his foreign policy initiatives.

---

[107] http://www.nytimes.com/2012/06/01/world/middleeast/obama-ordered-wave-of-cyberattacks-against-iran.html?pagewanted=all

[108] https://www.kingcounty.gov/safety/prepare/EmergencyManagementProfessionals/Plans/~/media/safety/prepare/documents/HIVA/Cyberterrorism.ashx+cyber+viruses+could+cause+radioactive+contamination&hl=en&gl=us&pid=bl&srcid=ADGEES j7YuiPtLyh1lOz2haZtXF5vJvQKJ-LkuPH8KUGKo7_znhCajy9LX _MfTOHIhQO4g1aHKTSsFbjzpTrSXwkcWEgzcUNUmNyQI _Zox4a91fjGkT4HiBtnFTKJEXAdCiu0N0d7r17&sig= AHIEtbSIk9qeTUkdX5uqoYxEGm7eUQXjCg

In Bahrain, for instance, the US acted against the best interests of the people to pursue what could be perceived as narrow US strategic interests. Libya and now Syria have not elicited personal intervention or attention from President Obama, and in the case of Libya, France's President Sarkozy led the consensus on intervention to support the liberation struggle. President Obama has been scant in his discourse on all the events and revolutions comprising the Arab Spring, and he has failed to make any policy announcements concerning the democratic revolutions of the Middle East except at a couple of critical points in Egypt's revolt.

When he did address the Egyptian revolution, President Obama highlighted concerns about the maintenance of law, order and respect for legally binding international agreements, because closure of the Suez Canal and any breach of the Sinai Agreement would have a direct impact on Israel. By including Israel in the protection of the Iron Dom anti-missile protection system and by initiating measures aimed at reassuring Israel over the Iran nuclear issue, President Obama has conclusively strengthened US commitment to Israel as its primary partner in the Middle East.

By far the biggest challenge to President Obama's lack of a Middle East strategy has been the killing of Ambassador Christopher Stevens and three other embassy staff on 9/11/2012 in Benghazi, Libya. The likely interpretation of this event will be to reemphasize the desirability for the US to have a concrete and longer-term Middle East stabilization policy.

Today, Russia and China are publicly questioning US policies and directly challenging the US on interpretation of international events and processes. The BRIC countries and South Africa have moved to strike a more independent line in foreign and economic policy, while some Latin American states like Ecuador, Argentina and Venezuela have taken up direct roles in creating a more balanced international power system.

The world moved from the Cold War to benevolent US hegemony after the fall of the Soviet Union. Today, nations are looking to recreate a balance of power. The reason is simple. Nation states do not want to be forced into supporting wars of attrition and interventions against other sovereign states under doubtful circumstances and without convincing and transparent information. This would nullify the global systematic of sovereignty on which the world currently operates.

The dynamics of the Arab Spring also introduces the specter of a new kind of political manipulation by the few (US, UK and a handful others): a new colonialism undertaken by financing insurgencies and internal destabilization; initiating war and then taking over the recovery process. Iraq, Libya and likely Syria are following the same model, and it is not yet known what will eventually happen in Egypt.

In August 2012, the meeting of the Non-Aligned Movement in Tehran delivered testimony that, in the era of mantras of regime-change, a majority of countries in the world want to support increased political balance in global politics and a multipolar global political order. The lopsided US support for its best friend and preferential partner Israel, and the perception by many that this relationship preempts all other foreign policy considerations for the US, is staying the hand of the US in foreign affairs, and undercutting confidence. Ironically, it creates abnormalities in the international political system and opens up space for multiple power centers to emerge.

The same anomalies prevail in Africa, where lopsided US support for Rwanda and its President Paul Kagame has led to the destabilization of the neighboring Democratic Republic of the Congo again. The US needs to take a concrete stand against Rwanda's expansionist designs on the DRC. If not, the prestige accrued by the US through AGOA will be seriously compromised. The DRC is in danger of disintegration and a return to full-scale conflict; the US holds the keys to resolve this issue conclusively once and for all, and the US must act soon.

The US-UK-French stranglehold on the UN Security Council over the last two years has produced another anomaly. The emerging confluence of Russia and China brings together powerful countries with formidable economies and economic potential. Russia and China are public in their willingness to oppose US strategy and policy on a host of global issues. Yet my analysis is that their overall objective is to balance, not bring down, US power in the international arena.

US policies have precipitated increased questioning of inherited power structures and decision modalities such as the UN Security Council, where five countries hold the power to decide who is an outlaw and who is a freedom fighter.

In an election year, as the global community looks back at Obama's term in office, there are lessons to be drawn and achievements to be chalked up. In the final analysis, President Obama gave the US results in their foreign policy. He has taken the US military out of harm's way in Iraq and likely to do so soon in Afghanistan; he has eliminated Osama Bin Laden and other key terrorist leaders, and he has defined an agenda of change for the next decades of US foreign and strategic policy.

President Obama has done all this in ways that are not acceptable to everyone and do not placate every country's politics. But finally, he has delivered the required foreign policy results that his nation needed, required and asked for. Only another four years of Obama will tell us whether his policies and strategies promote or constrain US global power.

Notes

The author drew the bulk of the information and references for this book from open source information provided in journals, newspapers and blogs. She also drew material and inspiration from material posted to her own blog and from comments made on these posts. Most of the maps are also open source maps that if searched on Google, can be seen on many different websites.

The author's blog can be seen at http://opinionscan.me

Introduction

1. http://en.wikipedia.org/wiki/New_America_Foundation
2. http://thecaucus.blogs.nytimes.com/2012/06/01/obamas-counterterrorism-actions-complicate-republican-strategy/
3. http://www.nytimes.com/2012/06/01/world/middleeast/obama-ordered-wave-of-cyberattacks-against-iran.html?pagewanted=all
4. http://www.csmonitor.com/World/terrorism-security/2012/0524/Pakistan-to-US-Respect-our-decision-to-sentence-CIA-informant
5. http://abcnews.go.com/Politics/osama-bin-laden-dead-president-obama-full-remarks/story?id=13506069#.UDo2fkKhDFI
6. http://www.iss.europa.eu/publications/detail/article/us-strategic-interests-in-south-asia-what-not-to-do-with-pakistan/;
7. http://www.thebureauinvestigates.com/2012/03/29/yemen-reported-us-covert-actions-since-2001/
8. http://en.wikipedia.org/wiki/Covert_United_States_foreign_regime_change_actions
9. http://www.foreignpolicy.com/articles/2011/10/11/americas_pacific_century?page=full
10. http://www.washingtonpost.com/wp-dyn/content/article/2010/04/08/AR2010040801677.html

Chapter 1: US Foreign Policy in the Middle East

1. http://gulf2000.columbia.edu/images/maps/Mid_East_Religion_lg.jpg
2. http://gulf2000.columbia.edu/images/maps/MidEast_Religion_and_Oil_lg.jpg
3. http://gulf2000.columbia.edu/images/maps/US_bases_in_Middle_East_lg.jpg
4. http://www.globalsecurity.org/military/world/gulf/rsaf.htm
5. http://www.nytimes.com/2012/08/27/world/middleeast/us-foreign-arms-sales-reach-66-3-billion-in-2011.html?_r=1&ref=todayspaper
6. http://www.bloomberg.com/news/2012-05-10/egypt-s-april-inflation-slows-as-food-price-increases-ease-3-.html
7. http://www.ibiblio.org/sullivan/docs/SinaiII.html
8. http://www.nytimes.com/2012/08/13/world/middleeast/egyptian-leader-ousts-military-chiefs.html?smid=pl-share
9. http://www.nytimes.com/2012/08/27/world/middleeast/egyptian-president-seeks-regional-initiative-for-syria-peace.html?ref=todayspaper
10. http://www.asecondlookatthesaudis.com/sitebuildercontent/sitebuilderfiles/asecondlookatthesaudisaglobalagenda.pdf
11. http://thegreatchessboard.wordpress.com/tag/jihad/
12. http://www.nysun.com/foreign/saudi-royals-mask-a-jihad-agenda/52999/
13. http://www.independent.co.uk/news/world/middle-east/gulf-keeps-close-watch-as-saudis-hold-union-talks-with-bahrain-7746869.html
14. http://www.independent.co.uk/news/world/middle-east/deal-with-saudis-to-shore-up-bahrains-repressive-regime-7743529.html
15. http://www.independent.co.uk/news/world/middle-east/deal-with-saudis-to-shore-up-bahrains-repressive-regime-7743529.html
16. ttp://en.wikipedia.org/wiki/History_of_Bahrain#Treaties_with_Britain
17. http://en.wikipedia.org/wiki/General_Maritime_Treaty_of_1820
18. http://en.wikipedia.org/wiki/Perpetual_Truce_of_Peace_and_Friendship
19. http://en.wikipedia.org/wiki/Bahrain_Petroleum_Company
20. http://en.wikipedia.org/wiki/United_States_Fifth_Fleet
21. http://en.wikipedia.org/wiki/State_of_emergency

22. http://en.wikipedia.org/wiki/Bahrain_Independent_Commission_of_Inquiry
23. http://security.blogs.cnn.com/2012/05/11/u-s-resumes-arms-sales-to-bahrain/
24. http://en.wikipedia.org/wiki/Bahraini_uprising_(2011-present)
25. http://www.nytimes.com/2012/08/01/world/middleeast/bahrain-criticized-for-torrent-of-tear-gas-use.html
26. http://physiciansforhumanrights.org/press/press-releases/bahrain-uses-tear-gas-as-lethal-weapon.html
27. http://en.wikipedia.org/wiki/Iran—United_States_relations#1977.E2.80.931979:_Carter_administration
28. http://www.hrw.org/news/2012/03/01/iran-fair-vote-impossible
29. http://www.foreignaffairs.com/articles/137731/kenneth-n-waltz/why-iran-should-get-the-bomb
30. http://www.algemeiner.com/2012/09/03/talk-on-iran-'red-lines'-comes-after-u-s-general-distances-himself-from-israeli-strike/
31. http://www.bloomberg.com/news/2010-05-31/israeli-s-diamonds-are-dubai-s-best-friend-as-profit-trumps-emirate-policy.html
32. http://en.wikipedia.org/wiki/Israel_Military_Industries
33. http://news.xinhuanet.com/english2010/world/2011-06/20/c_13938425.htm
34. http://news.xinhuanet.com/english/world/2012-07/28/c_131743749.htm
35. This section as many others in this book are drawn directly from the author's blog. http://opinionscan.me/2012/08/05/the-truth-about-syria-regional-spillover-and-theories-of-conflict-causes/
36. http://en.wikipedia.org/wiki/Rafic_Hariri
37. This information was received over a period of a year or so by the author from Syrian ex-colleagues that lived in the communities that were approached by Saudi Arabia and that participated.
38. http://www.nytimes.com/2012/07/25/world/middleeast/al-qaeda-insinuating-its-way-into-syrias-conflict.html?pagewanted=all
39. http://www.nytimes.com/2012/08/05/world/middleeast/turkish-alawites-fear-spillover-of-violence-from-syria.html?pagewanted=all
40. http://www.csmonitor.com/USA/Foreign-Policy/2012/0630/Not-much-progress-at-Geneva-meeting-on-Syria-violence
41. http://blogs.voanews.com/breaking-news/2012/09/04/us-nears-deal-for-1-billion-in-egypt-debt-relief/

42. http://www.nytimes.com/2012/09/05/opinion/egypts-economic-struggle.html
43. http://www.nytimes.com/2009/06/04/us/politics/04obama.text.html?pagewanted=all
44. http://www.nytimes.com/2012/09/03/world/middleeast/us-is-weighing-new-curbs-on-iran-in-nod-to-israel.html?ref=world

Chapter 2: US Foreign Policy in Near East and South Asia

1. http://www.guardian.co.uk/global-development/poverty-matters/2011/jul/11/us-aid-to-pakistan
2. http://www.fas.org/sgp/crs/row/R41856.pdf
3. http://www.nam.gov.za/background/history.htm
4. http://www.foreignaffairs.com/articles/138009/andrew-j-nathan-and-andrew-scobell/how-china-sees-america
5. http://www.whitehouse.gov/sites/default/files/2012.06.01u.s.-afghanistanspasignedtext.pdf
6. http://blogs.suntimes.com/sweet/2012/05/us-afgan_strategic_agreement_r.html
7. http://www.consilium.europa.eu/uedocs/cms_Data/docs/pressdata/en/ec/130285.pdf
8. http://www.chicagonato.org/chicago-summit-declaration-news-40.php
9. http://www.tradingeconomics.com/india/gdp-growth
10. http://www.upi.com/Top_News/Special/2012/04/02/India-upgrades-submarine-fleet/UPI-42081333372730/
11. http://www.worldpoliticsreview.com/trend-lines/11373/global-insider-despite-outpacing-competitors-indias-navy-seeks-to-upgrade
12. http://www.navytimes.com/news/2012/02/ap-india-upgrades-its-military-with-china-in-mind-020812/
13. http://www.nytimes.com/2012/09/05/world/asia/india-and-china-agree-to-resume-joint-military-exercises.html?_r=1
14. http://www.nytimes.com/2012/09/03/world/asia/in-afghanistan-hitting-pause-on-local-police-training.html?pagewanted=all

Chapter 3: US Foreign Policy in Africa

1. http://www.agoa.gov
2. http://www.africom.mil
3. http://www.globalsecurity.org/military/world/para/lra.htm
4. http://en.wikipedia.org/wiki/Ash-Shabaab_(Somalia)
5. http://www.crisisgroup.org/en/publication-type/media-releases/2012/africa/dr-congo-open-letter-to-unsc.aspx
6. http://www.haguejusticeportal.net/index.php?id=9467
7. http://www.provincenordkivu.org/doc9/Rapport_des_experts_des_NU_-_annexe_-_Addendum_(26_June_2012)FINAL[1].pdf
8. http://www.chicagotribune.com/news/sns-rt-us-congo-massacresbre87s0uy-20120829,0,6457089.story
9. http://www.scribd.com/doc/97990059/UN-DRC-Group-of-Experts-Interim-Report-21-Jun-2012
10. http://www.miningweekly.com/article/drc-gold-miner-declares-commercial-production-2012-08-29
11. Hutu perpetrators of the 1994 Rwandan genocide
12. Gerard Prunier *Africa's World War: Congo, The Rwandan Genocide and the Making of a Continental Catastrophy* Oxford university Press 2009, New York.
13. http://en.wikipedia.org/wiki/First_Congo_War
14. http://en.wikipedia.org/wiki/Second_Congo_War
15. http://en.wikipedia.org/wiki/National_Congress_for_the_Defence_of_the_People
16. http://www.scribd.com/doc/97990059/UN-DRC-Group-of-Experts-Interim-Report-21-Jun-2012
17. http://www.bbc.co.uk/news/world-africa-15317684
18. http://www.armytimes.com/news/2012/02/ap-us-troops-fighting-lra-in-4-african-countries-022212/
19. http://www.washingtonpost.com/wp-dyn/content/article/2010/07/12/AR2010071200476.html
20. http://www.usatoday.com/news/world/story/2012-08-23/uganda-somalia-unrest/57238980/1
21. http://www.bdssouthafrica.com/2012/02/sa-pledges-support-for-palestinians-mel.html

Chapter 4: US Foreign Policy in Europe

1. http://www.flickr.com/photos/normanbleventhalmapcenter/2710789398/
2. http://www.nato.int/cps/en/SID-5F2418B423EC9324/natolive/news_75177.htm
3. http://www.nato.int/cps/en/SID-5F2418B423EC9324/natolive/official_texts_72544.htm
4. http://www.bostonglobe.com/news/nation/2012/01/06/obama-outlines-new-military-strategy-focusing-asia-pacific-region-and-middle-east/bwYBkrOn6fyjzvWJliujWO/story.html
5. http://www.defense.gov/news/newsarticle.aspx?id=66706

Chapter 5: US, Russia and China: Shifting Balances

1. http://www.economist.com/blogs/easternapproaches/2012/03/putins-return?bclid=0&bctid=1485530842001
2. http://www.aljazeera.com/news/europe/2012/03/201231665525590255.html#.UD-duPuKXn0.gmail
3. http://rt.com/politics/russia-iran-sanctions-un-cooperation-us-268/
4. http://english.ruvr.ru/2012_06_21/78879876/
5. http://english.gov.cn/official/2010-12/23/content_1771603_6.htm
6. http://allafrica.com/stories/201201160075.html
7. http://www.fas.org/sgp/crs/row/RL34314.pdf
8. http://online.wsj.com/article/SB10001424052970203753704577254794068655760.html
9. http://www.foreignaffairs.com/articles/138009/andrew-j-nathan-and-andrew-scobell/how-china-sees-america
10. http://abcnews.go.com/International/wireStory/clintons-china-visit-produces-breakthrough-17156826#.UEjzTkKhBFI
11. http://www.quarterlyessay.com/issue/time-war-australia-military-power
12. http://www.voanews.com/content/us-australia-announce-expanded-military-cooperation-133955288/148258.html
13. http://www.nytimes.com/2012/09/07/world/europe/putin-calls-missile-deal-more-likely-if-obama-wins.html
14. http://geography.howstuffworks.com/oceans-and-seas/the-china-sea.htm

Chapter 6; Concluding Analysis

1. http://www.voanews.com/content/us-australia-agree-to-military-force-deployment-133946093/148236.html
2. http://www.nytimes.com/2012/04/05/world/asia/us-marines-arrive-darwin-australia.html
3. http://nhne-pulse.org/military-surveillance-swarms-of-cyborg-insects/
4. http://www.nytimes.com/2012/06/01/world/middleeast/obama-ordered-wave-of-cyberattacks-against-iran.html?pagewanted=all
5. https://www.kingcounty.gov/safety/prepare/EmergencyManagementProfessionals/Plans/~/media/safety/prepare/documents/HIVA/Cyberterrorism.ashx+cyber+viruses+could+cause+radioactive+contamination&hl=en&gl=us&pid=bl&srcid=ADGEESj7YuiPtLyh11Oz2haZtXF5vJvQKJ-LkuPH8KUGKo7_znhCajy9LX_MfTOHIhQO4g1aHKTSsFbjzpTrSXwkcWEgzcUNUmNyQI_Zox4a91fjGkT4HiBtnFTKJEXAdCiu0N0d7r17&sig=AHIEtbSIk9qeTUkdX5uqoYxEGm7eUQXjCg
6. https://www.kingcounty.gov/safety/prepare/EmergencyManagementProfessionals/Plans/~/media/safety/prepare/documents/HIVA/Cyberterrorism.ashx+cyber+viruses+could+cause+radioactive+contamination&hl=en&gl=us&pid=bl&srcid=ADGEESj7YuiPtLyh11Oz2haZtXF5vJvQKJ-LkuPH8KUGKo7_znhCajy9LX_MfTOHIhQO4g1aHKTSsFbjzpTrSXwkcWEgzcUNUmNyQI_Zox4a91fjGkT4HiBtnFTKJEXAdCiu0N0d7r17&sig=AHIEtbSIk9qeTUkdX5uqoYxEGm7eUQXjCg

About the Author

Zubaida Rasul-Ronning is a Canadian with roots in Asia and Europe, who has worked in international peacemaking, mediation and development for over 15 years for international organizations. An expert in the security sector and security governance reform, she has served on political teams negotiating and implementing peace agreements in Angola, Bosnia i Herzegovina, Guinea-Bissau and the Democratic Republic of Congo, and in development planning and management in North Africa, the Middle East, Djibouti and Somalia. Ms. Rasul-Ronning has a degree in International Business, from Thunderbird Management School (Arizona, USA), and a Masters in Human Rights, from Columbia University (New York). She is married and currently lives in New York City. Zubaida is now working as an international consultant while pursuing her interest in global political analysis.

www.ingramcontent.com/pod-product-compliance
Lightning Source LLC
Chambersburg PA
CBHW051442280526
45785CB00003B/1389